THE TELLING

To Schuyler, my husband, my partner in the endeavor to take words, and oneself, further — and, now, to outlive death's long moment . . .

and to my mother and my father, who imparted to me a durable sense of the further

Laura (Riding) Jackson

THE TELLING

UNIVERSITY OF LONDON
THE ATHLONE PRESS
1972

Published by
THE ATHLONE PRESS
UNIVERSITY OF LONDON
at 4 *Gower Street London* wc1

Distributed by
Tiptree Book Services Ltd, Tiptree, Essex

U.S.A. and Canada
Humanities Press Inc
New York

0 485 11137 3

Printed in Great Britain by
WILLIAM CLOWES & SONS, LIMITED
London, Beccles and Colchester

CONTENTS

Nonce Preface

[*Written for the presentation of* The Telling *in the magazine* Chelsea, *issue 20/21 May 1967, New York*]

The Telling *is a little book holding within its diminutive compass much that I know I could never have succeeded in saying while I was a poet: I was that until about twenty-five years ago. To speak as I speak in it, say such things as I say in it, was part of my hope as a poet. But, I have found, poetry imposes inhibitions upon the expressive faculties even while inducing expectation of new degrees of freedom of tongue, voice, mind, and all else that words live by. I was long in delivering mine from them after I discontinued the practice of poetry.*

My little work is a personal evangel. The reader of it here may wonder what it is doing among contributions to an issue devoted to the consideration of Science. It could be described as being also-present. Moreover, it was composed with conscious sensitivity to the subject of science. But it was composed with conscious sensitivity, also, to other subjects that have become underlined in the handwriting of our time; and, after not long, science disappears in it from the scene of my interest, as something not thought by me to be of frontal human importance. So, I offer some prefatorial paragraphs on the subject, for congeniality's sake, in my capacity as a contributor to this issue.

Much of what is called science none but scientists can or ought to talk about: this is an area of special operations, each concerned with a field of specialized knowledge — there can be contiguity between the fields, but no unions of them, or single union of all. The scientific Sum-of-Things (to use the term of Lucretius, who tried to make out of early materialist

1

philosophy a hybrid Truth, both poetic and scientific) cannot be added up! Or, to say it differently, in operational science there is room only for specialized knowledge. This is a satisfactory limitation where specialized knowledge is the object. And there would be no more to say if what is called science were operational science, wholly. However, science has for part of it a function of criticism, which it has assumed in the consciousness of its operational success — its progressive self-perfecting within its fields; it turns its face outward towards other forms of intellectual activity, those conducted in a field of general relevance, and transforms itself into an institution of general criticism. It can look very right, this criticism which science also is, because in applying principles of evaluation developed for the media of specialized knowledge in the medium of general knowledge it can make everything there look wrong. There is no substance, but there is method, behind scientific critical judgement: science functions as criticism by looking for its kinds of exactitudes in the general intellectual area, and, being without general measures, and so unable to determine the presence or absence there of exactitudes of a general order, attacking non-scientific operations as not meeting scientific tests. Since the character of the procedures of scientific general criticism is difficult to identify as what it is, its attacks tend to seem unanswerable.

People become dubious, often, of operations and positions they have maintained or favored when science (as criticism) casts its sceptic look at them, but without feeling themselves proved specifically wrong. Exposure to science's eyes-narrowed, hard-line, criticism sets their conscience's finger wagging at them: 'Haven't you been sloppy here, and there, or there, in your thinking ... your writing ... your checking on the subject of the words ... on the words themselves?' Indeed, there is frequently a case to be brought, where science levels its criticism, that it is incapable of bringing — that only those responsibly involved could, conscious of guilt, bring (against themselves). The power of scientific criticism lies in the effect of its master-accusation 'Nonsense!' on the intellectual conscience of those whose thinking it is, actually, powerless to evaluate.

What is the relation of this 'Nonsense!' to the little-magazine area of operations? This is an area in which, in principle, the strictures, the taboos, of conventional criticism are lifted, and blessings of freedom from them conferred: each individual operator is supposed to be acting on his or her critical own. However, there is danger, in any land of freedom — in little-magazine countries, as elsewhere — that the inhabitants will go very light — light to nothing — on self-criticism; governors, or editors, administering the freedom, may hint at the advisability of self-criticism, but cannot impose it. Most unfortunately, the criticism of science — the most sophisticated phase of it — leaves operators in the fields of literature and the arts, in their claims to professional prerogatives to deal in mystery, flatteringly alone, as engaged in 'emotive' activity — as doing something of a kind that people can't help doing, which has the justification of letting steam escape from the boilers of imaginative excitement. (In a major respect, also, the criticism of science is, curiously, tolerant of mystery: it allows in theory for an ultimate all-general ground of experience, but condemns attempts to attain to knowledge of it as necessarily productive of nonsense. Since science is not equipped for general knowledge, this can be regarded as a scientifically reasonable position.)

I think it can be useful, in a quarter where the usual hierarchies of criticism do not rule, to have, so to speak, a Science fiesta if science's general criticism is also invited along, to show its snooty face and leer its conscience-shaking 'Nonsense!' This unpleasant personality is a gift to all who operate, or think of themselves as operating, on the ground of general experience with better than commonplace knowledge of it. 'Have I checked the results of my operations for nonsense?' is the question it makes one rudely ask oneself.

3

The little work that follows is not by my authorial intention in any of the 'emotive' categories. But, as whatever it is read, it should be thought of as having been checked, not only directly for several, but indirectly for over sixty-five, years, for nonsense. As much absence of it as there may be I credit to a number of things. I cannot count critical (as distinct from operational) science as being of their company by more than formal attendance, but I have, nevertheless, something in the way of morale to thank it for. It is good to have there to look in the face.

OUTLINE

Life of the human kind has been lived preponderantly so far according to the needs of the self as felt to be the possession of itself. This self-claiming self is a human-faced creature, existing in the multiple form of a loose number reckonable only as 'the human aggregate'. The needs of this self issue from a diffuse greed, which is imparted from one to the other in garrulous sociality.

There is an alternative self, a human-souled being, a self conscious of ourselves who bear in manifold individualness, each singly, the burden of the single sense of the manifold totality. This self is implicated in the totality as a speaking self of it, owing it words that will put the seal of the Whole upon it. On what we each may thus say depends the happiness of the Whole, and our own (every happiness of other making being destined to disappear into the shades of the predetermined nothingness of the self-claiming self, which encircle it).

THE TELLING

|1| There is something to be told about us for the telling of which we all wait. In our unwilling ignorance we hurry to listen to stories of old human life, new human life, fancied human life, avid of something to while away the time of unanswered curiosity. We know we are explainable, and not explained. Many of the lesser things concerning us have been told, but the greater things have not been told; and nothing can fill their place. Whatever we learn of what is not ourselves, but ours to know, being of our universal world, will likewise leave the emptiness an emptiness. Until the missing story of ourselves is told, nothing besides told can suffice us: we shall go on quietly craving it.

|2| For science, the explanation of the first life-forms, or earliest matter-patterns, is a main end of knowledge. But the explanation of these cannot be the explanation of ourselves. My thought is that the explanation of ourselves can be the explanation of such mysteries — that in the missing story of ourselves can be found all other missing stories.

|3| Even those wait for the missing story of ourselves who have been taught to believe one of the customary stories in which we are accounted for, so long treasured as true and sufficient as to be lovable. The believers keep good faith with their story, thinking it enlarges their understanding because they believe it. But it envelops their

9

understanding in a cloud, and they become habituated to the gloom. They wait for untold truth to emerge from the story of their belief. They wait for light in veiled places.

|4| Everywhere can be seen a waiting for words that phrase the primary sense of human-being, and with a human finality, so that the words themselves are witness to what they tell. The waiting can be seen not only in the eager inclined posture of believers. It can be seen also on the faces of disbelievers, the idolizers of the evident: they are not happy in their impatient assurance of there being no cause but uncaused circumstance, they wear the pinched look of people whose convictions make them a meagre fare. In the eyes of all (in the opaque depths in them of unacknowledged presentness to one another) are mirrored (but scarcely discerned) concourses where our souls ever secretly assemble, in expectation of events of common understanding that continually fail to occur. We wait, all, for a story of us that shall reach to where we are. We listen for our own speaking; and we hear much that seems our speaking, yet makes us strange to ourselves.

|5| To tell one comprehensive story of how it has happened that what is is, one which shall hold true, come what may, now-after — a story that whatever comes shall perfectly continue or confirm: such is the ideal motive of religions. A religion addresses the longing in us to have that said from which we can go on to speak of next and next things rightly, in their immediate time — the telling of what came first and before done forever. Thus, a religion touches hearts more intimately than a

philosophy can, for a philosophy does not look back, or forward far, if at all, but stares hard at what 'is'. A philosophy would treat of all things, but succeeds in treating only of the appearance of things in its time: it is not a work of vision of mind, but of mind-sight only. It leaves vacancies behind and ahead, which are taken over on the one hand by history, and by poetry on the other. How our story has been divided up among the truth-telling professions! Religion, philosophy, history, poetry, compete with one another for our ears; and science competes with all together. And for each we have a different set of ears. But, though we hear much, what we are told is as nothing: none of it gives us ourselves, rather each story-kind steals us to make its reality of us.

|6| The weakness of history is that it begins late and ends early. It has neither old nor new to tell, but all is diminished in it to make the brief time of our learning that we are 'human' (without yet learning what it is to be *that*) seem half of eternity. Poetry leaves us otherwise lacking. The future-facing truth-telling that it promises our ears and imaginations never breaks forth from the tellers: the telling travels round and round the tellers in standstill coils, a bemusement in which tellers and listeners are lost. Teller, listener, story, become in poetry one bemusement, in which present and future seem to commingle, and the desire to tell truth and the need to hear it shrink from the touch of fulfilment in lazy unison. Poetry's numbered wording abbreviates truth to the measure of mortal premonition, which has but a midnight's reach. Poetry is a sleep-maker for that which sits up late in us listening for the footfall of the future on to-day's doorstep.

|7| Philosophy stops time, telling its story as if from eternity. But the voice of a philosopher is always the voice of *a* time. A philosophy is always meant to embrace the whole of what is to tell of the being of things and beings; but the philosopher's whole is always a mortal enlargement of a mortal part. Philosophers are concerned with speaking truth for their own minds' satisfaction, first; and therefore they are both seekers of knowledge and barriers to knowledge, to themselves, learning enough to soothe the pains of ignorance but not to overcome ignorance. The more generous they are with their wisdom, the wiser they will prove to be. But their wisest words, though we preserve them, do not *live*: such are not the words waited for.

|8| But I do not include in philosophy the new hybrid scientific-philosophic thinking, which, first, threw out the human substance in words and made them subject to a weird logic of physicality, as if we the speakers and orderers of words had died, all, but left the words behind; and then threw out (out of the domain of knowledge) philosophy itself, using against it to prove it foolish a false scientific sagacity in matters of words. Were language's own tests of logic applied to the utterances of the new, anti-philosophic philosophers, they would be in worse disgrace than that in which they have tried to put the old, proper philosophers. For they speak a jargon of mingled scientific and philosophic and ordinary parlance formed without the least aspiring desire to use words well: holding that it is from science that truth must come, they seek to speak, themselves, no more than axioms of scientific common-sense. But it was the uniform aspiration of the older philosophers to use words well, to think

to the mind's best, to employ the faculty of understanding, to which words belong as legs to the walking creature, or wings to the bird in flight, with an athletic zest in the intellectual exercise of their humanness. What has borne the name of philosophy in the ages is a grave strenuous sport in which the competitors strive to outdo one another in degree of truth attained. There is honor in it as a pursuit of intellectual excellence for the sake of the olive-crown of truth to be gained in the contests of the philosophic day — though not for truth's sake itself. The philosophy of the present philosophic day springs neither from love of the play of the truth-trial nor from natural love of the work of truth, which the Olympic feats of the philosopher-athletes leave undone. It is an abandonment of the functions of understanding to the uses of science, a reducing of the faculty of understanding to subservience to the processes of observation, which are the mind of science; it would make of science a supermind to our minds, with our minds. (And sometimes now, a scientist, pining for some old-fashioned philosophic generalization, to elevate him above the world of particulars, will make himself a brew of it — become himself a philosopher!)

|9| I pause thus lengthily over the scientific modernism of the philosophers of the new breed because it seems freedom from old stultification but is a new stultification, and a deliberate one. Such philosophers have no philosophy but a philosophy of intellectual self-pampering. They say, in effect, that our minds have been overworked. "Let us desist from trying to think further," their philosophy counsels, "and leave the explanation of the unexplained for *things* to make, to us." They invite us to listen for truth to what things report — 'things' in

the sense of material actualities; . . . to be content with the numerology of things as the way of wisdom, to equate knowledge of things with knowledge of ourselves, and the lore of things in their infinite numbers and variety of sums with truth. This thought-abridging philosophy of our time, dressed as it is in the language of honest, truth-loving incertitude, is a counsel of sin, and itself a sin. It is a scholastic form of the peculiar sin of our time, which is discontinuance of the journey to the meeting-point where beings have a debt to pay to Being in true words spoken of themselves to one another. To halt the journey before we come mind to mind (face to face in mind) with one another and lose the privileges of error that defective knowledge of ourselves confers . . . — this is an intel-lectual art-of-evasion (taught at the colleges), and a technique of action also, concealing final human irres-ponsibility in a showy responsibility of now. This Way may be found followed wherever the spirit moving minds is that of our treacherous time (not the spirit that does not vary, which urges on, or one of the spirits of former times that haunt minds, none of which is so self-contradictory as our time's own).

|10| In philosophy, and wherever else intellects ad-venture, lifeless systems, to take the place of live thought, are borrowed from science with reckless hand now, that we may be rid of pain of mind and travail of soul in our engagements with the unknown. The time, in love with easy knowledge and fast knowledge, has created a new materialism to minister to the appetites of the intellect. Human things are broken up into unreal pieces by this hasty learning-lust, studied in their supposed particulars at scientific remove; and in their reality they are far less

visible through science's glass than with the naked eye of human selfhood. The sciences that purport to treat of human things — the new scientific storyings of the social, the political, the racial or ethnic, and the psychic, nature of human beings — treat not of human things but mere *things*, things that make up the physical, or circumstantial, content of human life but are not of the stuff of humanity, have not the human essence in them.

|11| How can it be that there is both a waiting, everywhere, for true words of ourselves, and a not-waiting? . . . a hunger both kept pure, unprofaned by false satisfaction, and stilled with the taste of expedient alternatives to our truth? We are both purely and impurely ourselves: . . . purely, in that we are ourselves, and impurely, in that we do not know our whole nature, and live much in misknowledge of ourselves, part-corrupted into what we are not. Thus has it ever been with us. But we have reached the end of the possibility of self-ignorance, and can no longer draw on innocence to purge us of self-mistaking. We have come into full possession of the human inheritance. We have ourselves all in view and all within hearing; and to see ourselves false, and give and take false reports of the intelligence of ourselves sounding in our being, is only less than perversity and perjury by minims of honest slowness to see and know and tell aright while eyes and tongues and ears and minds, still, by custom, are apt in seeing, saying, hearing, thinking, awrong. We have a time-that-does-not-count of grace in which to cease our self-belying. We shall make our extremes confront each other, our unacceptance of the untrue and our acceptance of the false-true, and compel ourselves to stand with one or the other. The choice is a

foremade one, is in our words — in words: they admit no truth but truth. But ours the saying; and we have not yet said. Our truth waits for us as we wait for it. The time of grace has fined down into a seeming infinitude of less-and-less-time for the waiting. I think the change from this suspense of waiting-and-not-waiting will have come before it is perceived. Truth rings no bells. When we have corrected ourselves with ourselves, joined that of us which sustained us in false notions of our truth to that of us which sustained us in our waiting for our truth itself, we shall have the force of truth in us, and immediately begin to speak true. Later, we shall know that we have begun to speak true by an increased hunger for true-speaking; we shall have the whole hunger only after we have given ourselves the first taste of it.

|12| In the new finality of unfinality that is propounded in our doctrines of the latest fashion, there is a bond with the Oriental. We surrender ourselves to a Destiny capable of fulfilling only itself, that gives us only an ever-meanwhile of incomplete being to dwell in — to which we cling, foreseeing the reward of going the whole way, in the journey of being, as nothingness. A spiritual lassitude restricts our energies to minutiae, in myriads. What they of the Orient never had, passion for complete being, the ultimate curiosity, we are trying to lose. As, in the Orient, religions are philosophies in religious masquerade, our religions now become costumed philosophies: there is less and less future-focussed hope-of-self in them, more and more attempting to make friends with the notion of Stranger-Destiny, equated now freely and in loose reverence with the notion of God. That largeness of religion which was its proportionedness to the sweep of

the natural human desire to go to the end of self-littleness and the beginning of filledness-with-being, has been reduced to the petty compass of enlightened fatalism; new creature-comforts of self-importance are added to our human condition while final importance is taken away from it. But no single description serves to tell how we, the latest human beings, stand disposed to our being — I do not mean to imply in this passage that I think I am providing the whole contemporary tale of us with what I say in it. Yet it is so that we make together one Hesitancy: we feel an urgency about our being, and retreat from the margin of action to which it brings us. Much that seems entrance (at last) of human beings into the ultimate responsibilities of being is a suspicious moving-away from the culmination of our being; much that seems action is of the value of inaction. The disposition to being which is called 'existential', for instance, is a withdrawal of the self from the whole reality of being (rising around us like daylight impossible much longer to ignore) to the self's private reality of existence; it is a refusal of self to being, a suicidal self-salvation from the full of being (long sought — but the finding feared). We can the better see ourselves from outside this Hesitancy in which we are immediately enveloped if we consider the sense of the religions. For the religions have in some matters more understanding of us than we have ourselves, enlightened with historical intelligence (though in other matters there is only darkness in which glorified misconceptions shine starrily).

|13| The religious visions of what went before — of the All-Before — have excited the trust of people because their authors (the makers of the religions) labored at

vision: these were men of honest purpose. But they were especially men — they were man-minded, more man-minded than human-minded. They looked with the eyes of self-tenacious part-of-being, seeing a garbled whole-of being from their vantage of abstracted self; they were right with a twisted rightness, and narrowly imperious in their resolve that their visions serve as visions of the whole, and their telling as the truth of the whole. They, like their fellows in time, were but time-creatures, beings perpetuative of that contrariety-and-counter-contrariety into which Being broke — once, completely; they were men among men-and-women, members of a divided and sub-divided Congregation, relying on the percipience of their sex-kind as if it were pure human vision, and using their powers of self-insistence to enforce belief. They, undifferently from others alive in the past, were dwellers in dividing shadows, lone wondering beings for whom the joining light that outspeeds time flashed only sometimes, and only to be gone again. (They thought that *they* could seize the light and make it stay; perhaps they saw it flash more often than others, watched for it, and held the memory of its dazzle in their eyes between the flashes.) They offered more than they had to offer, in their wilfulness. They spoke in defiance of their not knowing well that of which they spoke. Their stories of the Before are both overfull and underfull, big with imaginative excess here, sagging from intellectual deficiency there. Yet, though their stories are not ones from which we can go on, but ones that — being taken for true — make us uncertain where next to turn, so that we stop, and beyond that only dream, they do us the service of stressing the main human necessity: . . . that we must know ourselves (what we are), to not-lose ourselves (know not self, but

ourselves). And they try to open to us the secret of ourselves — rather, to make the Secret open itself. If we
reflect on what the religions have attempted, we perceive
that it is something that we, not the religions, have to do.
But that there is something to be done, the religions
advertised all over time; and we of now, in our pausing
and pausing to do an endless less-than-something, may
renew our forward spirit by claiming for our own, as
from a treasury, the charge they took upon themselves. I
shall in a while, here, say more about them.

|14| In religion is much tiredness of people, a giving over
of their doing to Someone Else. But those who would
energize people by drawing them into political warfare
against religion are not concerned with having them Do,
Know, Be, their all—be all that humanness comports, know
themselves altogether, do their human everything. The
communizing counter-fanaticism is an effort to make over
what we are into not-ourselves, a salvation of the body from
the fumbling spirit in which *is* our humanness. Its
advocates would take away from us our deep natural
past, take us away from our creation. They present us with
an ancestry of shallow reach, a transparent depth of
yesterdays. They know nothing wrong but the wrong of
those yesterdays, and nothing right but to-day's correction of those wrongs. This is, indeed, this making-right,
as a casting-back of human-being into the Source where
First Things are, and an abstraction from it of a creature-
hood lightened of the ultimate human heritage: the new-
made life is a life of a repetitive same-day, a to-morrow-
less arrestation in the universe of a niggardly idea of
universal laws. This is a revolution not for the human
being, but against human beings. In the name of fellow-

love and compassion it visits hate and vengeance upon the fortunate; and within its locked universe — girdled with its Idea — good fortune cannot enter.

|15| We need to look closely at the doctrine of the unity of the proletariat — proffered as a deliverance of humanity from humanity; . . . not merely that we may resist its invasions of our world of diverse conditions the better, but mainly that we may learn how little different we are in the quality of our souls by not thinking as the doctrine's believers do. To them, the human archetype is the toiler, the abused; and the human story goes from old strife between social good and evil to a social state in which there is neither good nor evil, only a populace laboring under its own mandate (heaved with a single self-tyrannic voice) to perpetuate itself. The doctrine tears human beings away from the possibility of having memory of their utter, total origin, and awareness of self-fulfilments to be attained in the human large (beyond the little of the single self), and substitutes for the human large — for the gathered spirit we are, as we are human — a body-and-brain politic, with a life into which lives are fed to make the social eternity. But how do we, we who conceive of the human being as in archetype more angel of a universal mystery than risen animal playing a drama of social evolution on the stage of its race, bear ourselves towards our human condition? We idle in presumptions about ourselves that we do not either dare to abandon or attempt to justify. We build a new society round unprecedented aspirations for bodies and brains, awarding ourselves a fast-ascending best in the material niceties and physical magnificences of existence; and we leave our souls to their own devices, as if they were

strangers in the household of our being, guests with affairs of their own. We do not deny our souls: we acknowledge them, though with a vague, distant pride. But we neglect our souls, seeking them out only at moments of conscience-panic, to make sure that they are still there. And the neglected soul and the denied soul do not differ greatly: they pine in ghostliness, they belong more to our death than to our life.

|16| We can best defend ourselves against those who would crowd us all into a prison of shrunken destiny (planned in crabbed Occidental despite of loose Occidental hope and constructed in harsh Oriental despite of bland Oriental hopelessness) by knowing our missing story, and dwelling in it, as in the home of our thought. Let them move us to take our souls fully unto ourselves, and to speak from soul-self to one another as ourselves in truth: that speaking will be our story, and it will silence them. To defeat them we need only to tell our truth, which is theirs also.

|17| Our truth cannot be all-told, from the beginning told, unless we tell it to one another. But the memory-adumbrations of our utter, total origin have grown dim, dimmer, as we have on and on unanxiously promised ourselves that someone or otherone will some time or other time teach us what it wholly was. The dialecticians of the false historical truth which I have been trying to show in its mean reality in the entire human setting (this humanitarianism of a procrustean male sort) avail themselves of our silence to make their noise of argument-simulating-the-sound-of-reason. We prolong their successful imposing total forgetfulness of the past pre-

ceding all the pasts (the Great Past preceding all the little pasts) by prolonging our waiting to hear, deliver, know, our story, to the last possible indulgence of truth's tardiness, which is our own. And while they busy themselves as we bide truth's time, they, too, wait. They labor in a dead unseriousness, conscious of their poverty in truth, putting a solemn countenance upon their make-believe righteousness. They are but competitors in telling for the length of our too-long-waiting-to-tell. Let us turn from the doom they preach of us to matters affecting us all more deeply. What becomes of them and us belongs to a larger, older story than the tale of terror in which they have embroiled our present-time. We must brave this new extreme of human inimicality (a doubt of self turned against the Kind) in all our ways, but most by attending with a new thoroughness to our affairs of the spirit.

|18| But what do we know of the spirit? We do not know the spirit yet except in strangeness. And that is why it is a fumbling spirit: denied familiarity, it is with us no more than we allow, in our fumbling bodiliness (in which we reach towards it with some shrinking always, a fear of the flesh for itself). The very word is hardly ours, ours in the natural instant intimacy of words and their speakers (an intimacy of spirit!) . . . we are both vain of the word, and suspicious of its meanings of purer virtue, unwilling to engage ourselves mistakenly to be virtuous to a foolish extreme. But there is no possibility of mistake with virtue, no too-much of it. The spirit creates virtue out of that which it moves and, moving, makes become spirit. But virtue is only the step of transformation into spirit before the transformed *is* spirit; when the trans-

formed and the transforming are indistinguishable, thought and talk of virtue are irrelevant — virtue goes no further than short of spirit-fullness. In the word 'spirit' there is no moral tyranny, though it has old favor among us as a moral preen-word. It is the most active word we yet have among the words that report ceaseless being to our being (the word that is of all words, yes, the most quick with meaning!). It is worn meaning-thin from bold use, timid use, division between contexts of evil and contexts of goodness; but we must save it from ourselves for ourselves. For we have little enough with which to speak of life-in-the-great, which we know so far only as an immense shadow of life-in-the-small. When we speak of the spirit, and as of a reality, we speak better than we know. And, if we did not speak of it, lacking the word, our minds would tease our tongues till we did.

|19| If we do not call our great matters 'our affairs of the spirit' we may say 'our affairs of the soul'. But spirit and soul are of different speech-vantages. With 'soul' we look to the self-awareness, the self-possessedness, that fills (must fill) being at the utmost degree of itself (else it would, at its utmost degree, resolve into everlasting death); the soul is being imbued with the instinct of everlasting life, and the grace of self to consummate it. With 'spirit' we look to that single largeness which being has in its multipleness, that sameness which all that it is has because it is, and to the coursing between near-and-narrow and far-and-wide of all-being through itself for which 'nature' is too petty a term (even!), and 'love' (even!) too ineloquent, self-bound, a word. Or, spirit and soul can be thought of as base and apex of the living form

of being, and our affairs of the soul as the culmination of our affairs of the spirit — from which they arise . . . In soul, the forces of being unite; in spirit, they spread.

|20| Nothing simpler than 'spirit' can we say, except 'God'. And with 'God' we say only 'God', a name that covers over our ignorance of the way and the why of the spirit, and where and how it dwells.

|21| We say, in part-knowledge, that the spirit is within us. But how within? Not as if the lodger, and we the vessel, but as the whole, which cannot be outside the part. How can the part know in the whole the spirit within? This is not a religious riddle to guess, or a philosophical problem to ponder, or a logical exercise to dally with, but a question to which the human self must find a livable answer, one justifying the self-exceeding meaning of 'human'. To know the spirit within in the whole we must learn what we are in the whole, and be according to that, so that we know it in ourselves. And, as this knowledge-experience seems to me, while I study my human-mind's powers and wonder at those that lie at old rest amidst its advancing busyness, memory is the key: if, first, we remember what we in the whole were before selves were, then we shall have a First Knowledge upon which to found a later sureness, a recognition in ourselves of the spirit within as an indivisibility of ourselves. I propound that we have powers of utter recall hardly used, capable of yielding us the rudiments of spiritual knowledge — without which all we know dwindles perpetually to less-than-enough for truth's need.

|22| In every human being there is secreted a memory of
a before-oneself; and, if one opens the memory, and the
mind is enlarged with it, one knows a time which might
be now, by one's feelings of being somehow of it. In
describing the memory, I refer to what I find in me that
belongs to me not in my simple present personhood but in
my intricate personless identity with all that has pre-
ceded me to the farthest, timeless reach of not-me. A
like identity has each of us, reclaimable by the mind in
memory-form: I think I do not present a private fancy,
with this declared more-than-ancient thing of memory,
rather a common potentiality of imagining back to the
all-antecedent reality. I believe there to be a vestige of
the Before in our Now that each bears as an individual
mark, but that is, yet, the same mark, the same memory.

|23| Freud has seemed to trace a memory-line from
Present Confusion to an elemental Bodily Past; . . . and
to show a covered human animalism disacknowledged by
the immediate human self — which becomes (by this
premise) the captive of lies of its own purblind making.
Truth (by this premise) and its salvation-work begin in
the confession of atavisms, the theory of which, being
scientific-precise, has been taken for proof of fact. The
Freudian idea, from which our time has learned a view of
ourselves as possessed of a lower nature *not to be forgotten*, would oppose to the failures of spiritual analysis a
physiology of thought termed 'psychic', successful
according to its own standards of analytical honesty. But
the analysis is *psychically* only body-deep! . . . its honesty is a purposeful poverty in spiritual imagination . . .
the memory-line tunnelling towards a supposed explana-
tion-holding darkness is a short-cut to oblivion of the soul

— leading to the secretless cave of our bodies, in which can be heard only an echo-exaggerated physical gossip. I point to a memory that goes back beyond one's physical ancestors, and beyond the entire material ancestry of our bodies. Failure to capture it is but failure to pursue it with sufficient innocence: we need our purest curiosity for this remembering-enterprise.

|24| But, if by full memory-reach to the Before we attain a First Knowledge, this and our later knowledge will match and correct and confirm each other. Even, there is a simultaneity between new seeing of ourselves in the immediate and seeing back through ourselves to old being. In our various-being, one-being mounts to emergence from the ordeal of Difference called 'the universe'; and this now begins to be visible to us, though but faintly. And, as a One of ourselves counters, in tremulous appearance, the ubiquitous one and one of oneselves, and the vision ghost-like bars the individual thought-way of each, our minds hark back, or will hark back, to the sheer one-being in which by our bodies' measure we were as not but in which by our minds' measure we have, or shall have, a mirror-presence. We see, or shall see, an all-familiar One-image — our Before! And, returning from the memory, our minds are nearly our mind; and the One of ourselves we nearly know better than ourselves . . . Thus we become able to speak to one another as tellers of a living story, of the truth of which we are one another's surety. Such is the human fortune, readable in our very failures. We live a story that will not end if we begin it well. Other embodied being, besides the human, draws down upon itself an abbreviated fate; its fortune's span is a death's throw

from its beginning, a reluctant life-experiment. We, human, *are* life, an enthusiasm, being's own love-of-being outlasting Failure — an interminable faith in itself of the One-And-All.

|25| All creatures are of one beginning. All creatures less than human are creatures of manifold ends; being lives in them, but loses in them the way to the single end, where many-ness makes One and the Original Whole ceases to be belied in it. Is it not awesomely plain, if we look at the other creatures with the eyes of our difference from, and not our likeness to, them, that they fail to render being truly, in their diverse peculiarity — which we, as if monsters, adore as the natural? That *they* are speechless and *we* speak is the difference of truth. They could not speak it; and this is why they do not speak. If we do not speak it? We are then as they, with the difference of evil — a difference beginning in idle speech, culminating in falseness of word, that mocks our human distinction.

|26| Those who read here may better understand what I think of ourselves, human, by what I say of ourselves and the others, the creatures of limited being-range; there-fore, I shall pursue the comparison. They go none to an extreme, and so are none more than their bodies, though near-human seem some kinds in their bodily selfhood. We do not stop in our bodies, but outstrip them. We are more than our bodies, and can remember what was before them. *They* can have no memory of a Before; they remember nothing, only their bodies remember, and remember only things of the body. Being seeks, and shall find, its extreme in us. But they can afford no

finality except that of their insufficiency as embodiments of being. Not from them have we evolved, but from spirit's blind effort, called 'nature', to form perfect beings . . . in whom Being shall be recomposed, from its universal sunderedness. They are marvels, wondrous errors, creatures of accidental excellences, that astound; but we are creatures suffused with nature's whole intention . . . who must see for it, do for it, try to make ourselves what it has tried to make. I say these things of us not in praise. If this were all, which now we are, betrayers of the spirit, cheaters of nature, would best describe us. My wish is, in asserting our relationship to nature to be direct, and a primary one for it and us, to defy the legend of the closer identity with nature of the creatures of other life-walks. It is a foolish diffidence to think we are more strangers to nature than they. To think so seals nature in the envelope of the physical, and ourselves in an envelope of mental idiosyncrasy, as if we were offshoot-beings wrapped in ourselves, and spirit and soul but fancies of our alien condition interwrapped with us. Thinking so, we forget ourselves in nature instead of finding how we are the crux of meaning in it, and that the resolving of us is the resolving of it. Its memory of its purposes is in our keeping! We have the shape of its hopes! We must not abstract from it our humanness, which, most, carries its meaning.

|27| Now I shall try to thin away the mystery-semblance that the notion of a memory of a time before bodily, and even material, existence, must wear, till we meet the memory in us. How can such a memory be in us? Are not all memories stored in the body? How could the body hold this memory, which is a memory of the soul-being that

being all-was before physicality was engendered? The
steps of my thought are these. That first was a division
within the soul of being making never a mark, the parts
inwardly self-same, not numberable, countable; more,
this was, a doubleness of fullness, than a division — the
parts not moving apart, only repeating each the whole
soul's One in perfect simultaneous response to the other.
Then, division became overt. How could this be! A flaw
in Being? Yes, I think: . . . the flaw that it had not been
tried in any test of it! . . . no other. Even perfection has
need of proof — bears within it a need to prove itself to
itself; all dangers must be run for the perfect to be ever
perfect. And, of all dangers, those of contrariety — that
Being could in ways go counter to itself — lead: these are
the universal testers, all other dangers are but their
mimics (sometimes senselessly, sometimes evilly, so). My
thought has first in view, then, a division within the soul
of being like One with One identical, where One is all.
Next, the division becomes overt, individuation mounts:
exposed, now, the dangers of contrariety. And Being was
as lost from itself in a dispersion of itself in existences, that
ensued; and physical time, and the material condition,
were born; and an end was made of utter soul-being. The
memory we have in us of a time before physical time is
the memory of this end: our memory of utter soul-being,
possessed through the body's witness to what-has-
occurred, is a memory of its ceasing. First we remember
the Soul that was once utterly All as that which now
utterly is-not. (Haunting our knowledge, it points out to
us our souls.) We first discover soul-being in the memory
of the beginnings of bodily being, in which it ceased. (But
it would form again, changed!) So goes my thought. That
the subject of the creation should be so treated, without

leave from the theologies or sciences or philosophies, and bare of the benefit of narrative symbolism and the decoration of known names, and the protection of a Name of names, may seem a rash simplicity to you who read here. However, I am not endeavoring to excite belief, or regale the reading imagination, only to tell what I find to see where my thought takes me.

|28| Yes, I think we remember our creation! — have the memory of it in us, to know. Through the memory of it we apprehend that there was a Before-time of being from which being passed into what would be us. And the Soul was gone, that had been the entire Form of Life, become transmuted into formless spirit. But, spirit working where matter spread in Soul's place, and farther, into emptiness, dispersed being was contained in a saving possibility of *souls* — souls to fill Soul's absence with a new One-being, risen up out of plurality: . . . each soul shining the Form of Life on the other. (No, a *promise* of this. All that is to be, however, is mere possibility until it is.) For long and long there were no souls; there lived only bodies that were types of diversity, combinations of aspects of diversity exemplifying, more than unity, variety, of being. Souls there were not until there were bodies in which, each, diversity's extremes were brought into a union; . . . another and another and another, to that rounding-in and exhaustion of diversity which is human. Thus from physicality emerge persons — ourselves.

|29| We are physicality's ultimate response to spirit's working, we answer spirit's beseeching *with* spirit, we deliver up to spirit in the shape of ourselves the spirit within: thus is it possible for it not eternally to die in and

with its works, and have all to try and do again eternally, as from the beginning of numbered being. Such is the work of souls; and spirit finds its repose in them, and the Soul that was once Entirety is revealed in them as the single principle of each. But there *are* no souls, we do not *have* souls, except as we remember the Soul's before-being, in our bodily after-being.

|30| But let me not be taken to think that I provide an explication sufficient to all-dispel the haze of mystery rising from, clinging to, my conceptions of how it was-and-is. (I myself feel a presence of mystery-haze even at my words' best outspelling of my meaning.) Whatever I say cannot of itself suffice: that which I may make clear will soon be clouded over, unless my saying is multiplied by other and other saying . . . will be scarce-noted until my telling is joined by other and other telling to the point of perfect interreference, the sufficient mutuality. It must seem that I speak as one who deems herself a beginner in the telling of our story, a first to speak our truth in truth. Indeed, I do not address myself to this speaking-task as one taking a next place in the procession of advisers on what-to-believe, or how-to-think, which unendingly girds in our mental ranges. And I know none before me who labor at our story seeking to be moved by no other inspiration than that which moves them to be: with all before me, as they appear in comparison, some task-master doctrine, garbed in sublimity or wearing sagacity's uniform, intervenes by their own evocation between them and their being, so that they speak without free access to that of which they tell. Many such lordships stand athwart our speaking-paths, turning the spirit-flow from self to mind and mind to mouth out of its

natural courses; and truth is thus ever at a new remove, though each turn of the way is given the name of it. (Or, some make lordships out of the will of the tongue, which can work persuasions on the lenient ear that vie with truth in irresistibleness: the wayside storying of poets draws travellers from the truth-road, charming them with the confident appearance of being truth enough for as far as they have gone — and perhaps for further. But my thought in this passage is especially of the storying that sues for belief, or subscription, and both justifies itself with other authority and rears up its own.) I do not bar the way with Incontrovertibles; there is room in what I say for going onward — whether it be taken to mind or not. And I split Incontrovertibles barring the way, to make onward passages in them — admitting no necessity of turning aside.

|31| Some, reading here, may know earlier efforts of mine to clear a way for the storying of us. Perhaps in those I seem more graceful, and to go faster. I advanced then on the still wings of forevision of a time of telling true. Here I endeavor to advance into truth's actual time, the measures and harmonies and very progress of which we must make as we go. There can be no thought of the manner of the going, in our moving to break out of physical time, a continuity of ever-dying repetitions of creation . . . I speak, in these pages, to see what may be accomplished towards the telling of our story under a new time-sign, the sign of the completed creation. And better perhaps than to call this the sign of truth would be, to call it the sign of ourselves. If we can begin to tell the story of ourselves without the intermediation of patron-doctrines, themselves fear-exacting, between our fear-of-

truth and ourselves, and without resort to spells of passing truth-vision, conducive to body's-more-than-soul's
rapture, then what we tell must become, as we go, truth
increasingly.

|32| There have been things said of old, by persons
eloquently worshipful of some doctrine or divinity as the
very self of truth, that seem to have been spoken from
out of the familiar human bosom of being — for natural
rings the fervor of devotion to what fills the place of
truth. Things said of old, making the appeal of truth by
the force of fervor, and in the ever-favorable circumstances of an ever-unsatisfied need of truth, have been
borne along from age to age and land to land in the de-
scent and spread of belief, which, multiplied, multiplies
the power of the words, and swells them with the breath
of reverence to proportions of sacredness . . . It was asked
of me by one close, contemplating with me what has been,
of words offered as, and widely and in time upon time
taken for, our truth, how I thought Buddha ought to be
counted, who seemed to speak free of a master-influence
— whether a primary inspiration might not be claimed
for him. By his going among people as a lone meditator,
whose words served only his own mind's meaning,
Buddha could be counted free; but with him invisibly
went another, an autocrat-idol of Righteousness by
whose prescription Life itself was the Wrong, and Virtue
was to feel guilt-in-living, and absolution lay in the
surrender of the soul to a heavenly non-being. The words
of Buddha served the idol: from the idol his mind took its
meaning, though he spoke as with his own wisdom. (And
he became himself an idol!) Under the joyful name of
Nirvana was here magnified Final Irresponsibility of

being. Creeds empty of hope presided over his hope; envisioning Good in their shadow, he prophesied a perfection of human nature that was but the loss of it . . . But who, trying to tell how it is with us in regard to the spirit within, has spoken free of the assistance of Authority, in one or another of its mind-prompting forms? . . . spoken in mere faithfulness of individual being to Being, the Whole-of-us carried in our nature? . . . Though I fail here, I cannot utterly fail. In what I say, there is no authority to defy, refute, destroy: it is itself only. It is a start. If it fails, it will still be a start. (Not a false start: the false starts — and I have made some — look too eagerly ahead . . . and soon, then, behind, it is as if nothing had happened, no start had been made. The start I make here stays with itself . . . and I, with it.)

|33| The stories of our souls in which our man-magisters have variously schooled us, from backward human childhood to this precocious senescence of the present, are all adulterated with lessons in allowances and deprivations and rewards and penalties and all the other equipment of rule. Every spiritual story told has been armed with an over-system making belief imperative — as if that were truth which best imposed itself. Even in our most generous stories, the cost of unbelief is destruction. Of how many theories of souls are we the prisoner-subject! Does truth make free? I think free makes truth. But not that free of modern-mindedness which disembarrasses thought of the idea of the soul — so that we define our troubles narrowly enough to put cures within reach, and treat the Rest as a vortex of unreality from which to keep a safe distance; and a sickliness of word settles into our serious speech, and Whimsy sobered with Common-sense

or Common-sense aflare with Whimsy (the difference is immaterial) is the spiritual style of the up-to-date hour. If there is talk of the soul, the talk is a soft elegance round a stony core of concern with the moment-to-moment self; our spiritual practicality is the gambler's choice of a continual moment-to-moment saving of ourselves, with souls-saving following in its wake as an obsolete alternative. *This* free could be the ultimate prison. For selves apart from souls have no life of their own. The body suggests the self, but only the soul can lift the self out of tenebrous physicality into the common light of being. To save ourselves we must save our souls: to save ourselves we must *find* our souls . . . But, speaking so, I mean no danger-cry; nor is it my purpose to urge . . . To the telling-place I bring some story-efforts of *my* being's own soul-being. (For story-efforts there seems enough soul-being in me; and this much ought there to be in each.) It is not the place we know, the stage of public recitation on which the competitions for our belief are enacted; it is a confiding-place, a reminding-place, a place for the speaking of all with one another in the privacy of human recognition of one another. I do not despair, though I find myself in a solitude: the place, not mere company, is the first necessity, in such speaking. Since I am not at work, in what I say, to prove myself, or what I say, but to open the question of our proving one another, in what we say, I have no anxiety or impatience apart.

|34| I must return to my talk of the memory of what was before every before ! The summary of my ideas on this subject is:— to have the memory is to have a soul. With the memory, we *are* soul, besides being body. Without it, our minds, however agilely they work, cannot be more

than servants of our bodies; with it, our minds can make our bodies, soul-subdued, accompany and sustain them in *their* work. Mind is the reason of all-being — which, once of one presence with being's one Soul, was loosed into the universe in which the Soul was dissolved — gathering in *beings*. Where there is body that is the universe drawn into a littleness living beyond its great cycles of change, each such littleness has a destiny of enlargement: Soul in-little and Mind in-little await such body, as the means of presence. There is a readiness in the Spirit of being for our being All . . . a multiple One! Our souls and our minds are like First and Last self-forms existing in one time; in them, body-joined, Before and After touch. This is the human condition — but not 'human' as spoken with that presumptuous familiarity of indulgent contempt of ourselves with which we god-like look down on us from the heavens of common-sense. The human condition is a readiness in us for a reunion of being in ourselves (even that readiness for our encompassing all-being which is in the Spirit). The work of our minds is to know that a reunion of being can take place in ourselves; . . . that we have All to be, all to do. We must think our way into our condition in order to know *what it is for*. And, where knowledge fails, we must go back to remember.

|35| What I have just said is (I know!) like something that the five fingers can barely cover rather than something that the hand can take into itself. What is this *mind* I now introduce into the count of our components? Of soul, spirit, matter, body, I have spoken as if a story of our being intertwining the themes of these four might be a sufficiency. Mind seems to be nowhere. Is it but a

nothing that has a name, a genie imagined doing our
bidding? I have said it is the reason of being that was with
the Life-Soul in which being moved all as one; and then
reason went with the spirit, when the Soul passed (dis-
appearing) into it. As spirit was formless, reason was formless; and, while spirit worked, reason rested, rested, and
Thought was Futurity; and all sense there was in the world-
in-the-making — even to the latest world-phase of the
universe antecedent to the human, when the making will
be fulfilled — was adduced backwards from final ought-to-
be. Not mindlessly travels the world through its phases.
While reason rests, rests, mind — in a mutual bounden-
ness of reason and spirit to each other — keeps a watch;
mind is the watch reason keeps, the watch spirit, by
reason's following attendance, keeps, on its works. And
mind translates the *not* of the world's successive states of
incompletion into *not-yet*, *not-yet*, until ourselves are,
and completion is, in us. Mind, then, is contained,
becoming our minds — and these, by our calling on them
for our truth (as on ourselves perfected!), become as our
mind in each. No one's was mind before we were: reason
had no home after the Life-Soul ceased, except Tem-
porariness. — Oh, shall we not command ourselves to
take the watch? From the watch we shall rise to *do*, when
spirit in us reaches its utmost, and can no more: we shall
give reason action, and give spirit rest. We shall live as
souls, and endure as minds; and our bodies will perpet-
uate us as ourselves, in the new being. Everything will be
taken along, in the new being, except what belies it.
Thus, in the very telling of our story to one another is the
crux of salvation: as we speak it true, we *have* new being,
and are in the new time . . . Where, when is that —
marking time from now? Where, then, is now? To ask so

is to tarry in the old time. There is no answer outside the story of us, true-told by us to one another; and we shall cease to ask, as we tell. I myself, speaking of such truth and, at once, attempting to open the door to it (which cannot be opened except from the other side — but this is only a way of saying that the thing is not done till it is done), stand as in no-moment, turn to and from and to the told-of telling, and make no count of time. We shall have certainty of our being in the new time not when we can prove that we are in it, but when it proves itself to us to be that: it will shine a new light upon us, and we shall see the cause to be in ourselves.

|36| Quickly to return to thought of the Life-Soul: it must be brought within our story's conscious compass, if we would have our story reach to the ultimate new; our telling must go back to the absolute oldness of being, for word of an absolute newness to be true.

|37| The memory of the Life-Soul slumbers in the human, then part-wakens as there begins to speak in us a knowledge of ourselves *as* human, which is to say, as beings whose bodies belong to their minds, and whose minds, to the remade Life-Soul, thinking by them in us. (Or, as ourselves here, in whom, from the outstrewn life of Being that spaces the universe, the original fact of Soul returns to itself, and again — possessing and possessed by us — is.) There is need of tending that memory: it is as a root by which knowledge of ourselves can rise to its full. And in the fullness of the knowledge will be proof of the rememberer, and, so, of the memory. The interaction of the memory and the knowledge is a mutual enlivenment! . . . But for very long to *remember*

and to *know* were too far apart in us to interact with keen force. Even, the memory, pictured so large in the stories of the religions, distracted from the desire of the knowledge. The religions have magnified the Life-Soul beyond the powers of memory, and belittled the knowledge of ourselves who recreate it with ourselves; they turn our eyes on ourselves, then turn them fast away; they help us to find ourselves, then lead us away from ourselves. There has been too much leaning on Soul-memory in the religions, and not enough seeking of an immediate knowledge of our being, a whole sense of our immediate being, a full knowledge of ourselves. This is the reason why always in the stories of the religions there is a break between past and present; the stories do not reach into the present, and reach over it only into futures that grow instantly old at touch. But beware of parting from the religions as if we could truly live without living according to the true story of our being, or as if there were nothing to tell except tales of scientific surmise — which we might eke out with the spiritual dilettantism of our choice.

|38| In this time, when all our true questions, that have wandered off to strange answer-lands, come home in beggary, beware of offering them for lodging the new plausibilities that have been added like temporary outbuildings to our House of Truth (in which we dumbly skulk, ghostly caretakers seeming in an unreal absence of ourselves). Open the doors of the House to them, let them populate its silence, lay their crusts on the empty board: some charity of the religions will have remained with them, and, feeding on this, they will rededicate the House to its forgotten function ... Not otherwise shall

we effect presence in it . . . The religions confirmed our consciousness of there being a First (an utter first) to remember. We must beware of parting from them in bad faith — denying that consciousness in defiance of them.

|39| The way in which religions come to be can be read in our still uncompacted human-nature. Memory-of-the-Before works in us separately from knowledge-of-the-Now, competing with it for our mind's care; and sometimes the one leads (though we might scarcely think it is what it is), and sometimes the other. And, in our nature's total course, against the press of Now, Now, Now, rises the protest Once, Once, Once; and this becomes someone's unique impassionment . . . Sometimes in someone rises a passion of resolution to speak of Before, and to remember enough to speak true; and round this passion forms a religion. The religion-making part falls to the one who cannot avoid playing it. Then, as a flock of birds suddenly drops to a tree to break the journey, listeners to the story are there, purpose and chance indistinguishable in their attendance.

|40| To some degree, all the religion-makers have a madness in them. They lay upon themselves as a command the common need of a faithful account of what it was that passed into what is: they let the need take possession of them, using it upon themselves as a goad, forcing from their sense of the Remote too-vivid remembrances, child-tales of a dreadful earnestness. They make the disquiet of others their own, and appoint their own disquiet a messenger to bring from Before-being the word that allays. The madness in them is their thinking

that their single acquaintance with Before-being can suffice as the single equipment of all our truth. They live, by imagination, more in the Before than in the Now-After, endeavoring to find in their memory-of-the-Before the better knowledge of ourselves (as if in its Then were the revelation of our Now). To these hungerers after perfect, actual memory of the Before, the Before seems the greater part of Our Life, the main matter of our story. It is thus with them, I think, because they are over-strong in sensitivity to the former fact of the One Soul that came before souls, the One Being that came before beings; . . . and over-strong in this because they are weak in sensitivity to the potential fact of the One we may be, that knocks continually at the doors of the ones we are (which, if opened to the knocking, are, most, soon closed, as if it had been fancied). They dwell too much on the Before, which is not to be recalled in the manner in which are yesterdays: they take it too much to themselves (man-like), as if it were a property — and impose on their memory of it a borrowed lively detail of antique recency. And they dwell not enough on the Now-After. But let us be grateful to the religion-makers for their wild will to remember in the large, and speak true in the large. The voice of such effort to attain certitude in the knowledge of being by *will* has made the voices of many on many throb responsively in their throats; . . . which has eased the anguish of mute groping for a vision of the First clear enough for true words to be spoken of it (in beginning of truth). We have borne the waiting without madness through the religious passion of a few.

|41| But for the religion-makers the human air would daily crackle with an intolerability to us of our daily

speechlessness on first and last things. They have done right to speak out on first and last things, though wrong to speak of them as if they saw them in the whole — since the whole is part-darkened for them with the colors of their mortal Now. And we have done right not to speak out in our incertitude, and wrong to stand in our own light, so that we could not speak out without error. Against their over-precise stories of Before, ending in obscure Afters, we have set nothing but unspoken wonderings, or careful speculations written for us, that we can say and unsay with the flow and ebb of the tide of Opinion. But their and our wrong of doing and not-doing are one; their wrong and their right go together (as do ours), and we have taken it all unto ourselves, and what there is to be forgiven is to be forgiven as to ourselves.

|42| Those who have no gentleness for the religions are the same who tell of us "And there was first Nothing." They use the errors of the religion-makers, who begin their telling of us with Something, to justify their articles of unfaith. Whatever has worth, they teach, even to our very selves (souls, they do not concede us), is something wrested from nothing. They make themselves out to be devotees of human community, and deniers only of 'God'. But they deny *us* more than they deny 'God'. For human community is an active mutuality of souls in which the countenance of what first was is revived . . . Let there not be any ceasing of thinking 'God' without thinking into the heart of the ignorance with which the notion of God is substanced. It is a notion at its origin-point alight with truth, articulate with memory of a First known as a Life-Soul, though dark with

confusion in the accounting for the later Spirit, and then ourselves. There is a manner of abandoning the notion that can be an abandoning of ourselves.

|43| I do not like it that I caution and counsel so much, here, rather than only tell my story of us. This is to speak louder than story-speaking, in which we are as in the same room with one another. It is as to cry at listeners across world-distance. But we are only a little, yet, as in the same room with one another — the room of our speaking at close ear to one another comes and goes. Much of what we have to say — though all is matter on which to put heads together — must be spoken with weighted reverberance, to be heard; and one may sound, saying it, as if one thought oneself the others' voice of conscience, come from the keeping of 'God' . . . But in all that I say, of storying or cautioning or counselling kind, I yearn to do better ! . . . to speak, whether for another's and others' near or far hearing, not for their hearing alone, but for their speaking as well . . . your speaking. Do *you* speak, and *you* . . . making our subject less mine, more yours . . . less yours, more ours. And we shall then be not merely as of the same room, but, in real meaning, of the same Subject, and Soul. I yearn, more than that I do better, that we do better.

|44| The difficulty of telling the story of us is, greatly, in the timing of the telling. It must be timed to us: we must tell it in our *last* Now, in which we are at last ourselves, come to the end of the making of us. It has been told — mistold — Now, Now, Now; and, mistelling it, living by it mistold, we have somewhat ever unmade ourselves. When we are in the story, it goes from its first Then to

our Now without break. When we stand somewhat outside the story, the subject seems 'God'; and, trying to tell
ourselves back into the story, we turn it into two stories.
The urgency to make one story of the story of God and
the story of ourselves cannot unite them, only lose the
second in the first; for the notion of God divides Before
from After, keeps a difference between Then and Now
never to be overcome . . . not ever in this way of telling.

|45| 'God' takes the story of the Life-Soul that dispersed
itself as spirit to a point of partial reunion, partial
restoration of Being's One-being. Calling on 'God' speaks
the wish of men that the cycles of disunion die in us, as
we are men and women living out the war of men with
men. But the cycles of disunion have their nexus in us as
we are men and women living out the whole unmaking
of being and remaking of it in ourselves as men and
women. And what we have to do is not for 'Man'
(which includes 'Woman' counted Nought) or 'God',
and not for ourselves, but is for Being. Being, which was
first ever all-one, waits to be made all-one again, through
our being: it waits for our souls to recreate Soul. And
what is God, according to such storying? — it is men's
hope of themselves enkindled by the love, of them, of
women, who have made their plights of anger, despair,
vanity, self-despite, their own. To the hope of *one
another*, which is Being's hope of itself, God is a rival to
be dealt with generously.

|46| When we take the memory of First Things, which is
ensconced possessively in the religions, into our own
hands, and retrace our beings to where we know Being in
them, the difference between Then and Now will vanish

in a joy of being ourselves for Being's sake. But let us keep a kindness for the shrines of religious memory, in which we seemed caressed with the breath of Before-being. It is better to have suffered the humiliation of mis-belief — its fervent confusions of utterance or silence — than to have opinionated on what was and is and is to be with memory choked off and imagination frowned down and reason stiffened to an incapability of being reason-able . . .

|47| Most mute, as rememberers of First Things and per-ceivers of Last Things, and knowers of ourselves as that in which First and Last are bound together, are women. To speak of this is to broach a story within the story of our-selves! I have a few times here looked towards this story, and just now I borrowed from it (in talking of God). As I approach the end of this communication I venture onto the ground of it, looking towards the larger story from there. It is fitting that I close my speaking on this ground, within the borders of which we live still, our beings compressed to part-size.

|48| Our sexuality is the record, and the obstinate process itself, of antagonism (sprung up of first-old *in* being, in the repetition of One in One) countered with counter-antagonism throughout time's numbers, to the turn in time, and numbers, where being ends the exploration of multiplicity and begins the repossession of its unity. In the turn, the human quality of being — before, hovering like a collective dream over multiplicity — becomes immediate; . . . becomes ourselves *fitfully*. The reality lives, we are human at whiles, we are men and women risen out of this twofoldness (legacy of Division) into a

onefoldness of knowing One in one another. — Then the recognition is gone! At the turn in time where being turns human, sexuality over and over plays out the pre-human, the drama of numbers. Hardly is the turn rounded.

|49| The man-part of ourselves, harborer of the force of antagonism come from time's beginning seeking an end, over and over seizes time in its turning, postpones, postpones, the human beginning, the beginning of the universal reconciliation. The man-part of ourselves speeds and delays, desiring to be both *its*-self and *our*-self; and, to this self-doubling, the woman-part of ourselves is made captive; and the Last Things are not lived, only talked of.

|50| And the woman-part of ourselves, harborer of the force of kindship (I use this old word to go beyond the softer, lighter, meaning of *kindness* to a meaning of making-one-kind-with, by the painful work of feeling the likeness of the different) — how, when, does the captivity cease, the woman-part become free? Through an instant readiness, eternized by the woman-part in itself, to pass beyond kindship to oneship (to eternal humanship) when the man-part, knowing itself at last its own prisoner, ceases to love the half-world formed of its self-doubling — in which both parts huddle — and calls for the whole. Foresense of Being-made-whole-in-us sits secret in women, in the mute mind of their kindship; and they listen for the call with this, and with this will hear it — even above the clatter that rises from their garrulity of heart (which is but a cheerful defiance of free souls offered to their confinement). And they will respond

to the call from another world, go to another world, to speak, that will be whole, because of their responding, and because of the calling. They will have risked the other world's being not whole, not anything — and the half-world lost. Thus shall the woman-part and the man-part make each other free; thus shall we, men and women, locked in the intricacy of being men and women, free ourselves to be ourselves.

|51| This going to another world, that it is in women's fate-life to attempt, and, attempting, accomplish, will be only a brief journey — a journey into an unknown to their hearts well-known. All the steps but one have, indeed, been taken by them. Only not taken has been the step of the mind. When women take their step of the mind out of the world that, less than a world, has been at most a mirror made of nature by man-minds for men's justification of themselves to themselves before their eyes — we shall not, then, be all in a mirror-world created by woman-minds, but in the place of the Whole, where for every being who would be according to the Whole (would be a being of the Whole — one of One) is a whole mind, a complete gift of reason. The minds of women are not, as seems, either partners or competitors to men in the reading of the mirror of the self. It is through mere love that they live according to men's self-reflecting half-world, preserving their woman-selves to men's longing to be themselves and preserve themselves from themselves: their love, fed upon the praise and favor of men, is of that world, but not their honor. And men will be preserved neither by their own self-love nor the love of women, but by the ultimate honor of women, the prior motive of their souls, and the principle of their

minds — put by fate ever and ever out of harm's daily way into Reason's last keeping.

|52| No further can go the man-minds. They have reached the half-point, the finality of divided being; and their every further step makes only a new imprint in nothingness. These minds were borrowed from their humanness — or so it pleased them to believe. These minds were facsimiles of the not-yet-possessed originals waiting for them beyond the self-limit: they had the name of human minds on the title-page, but the contents were blank, and all the man-thought written upon the pages began to vanish as soon as written. Women have tried to think by such mind-books, such man-thought; but they know little happiness in fashioning semblances of truth, with nothing surer than fame to gain.

|53| Women have mainly awaited the time of the Claiming — when men would call for the total common indivisible human inheritance from Forever. It being in the fate-life of men to abandon their half-world, half-truth, half-thinking (which, doubled in the passion of self-fullness, makes not a whole, but brimming nothing) at the point of empty wholeness, and there to ask the Whole, for itself, intent and pure must be the listening of women for the note of pure desire, for the cry of true need — Being's need as Our need — rising above the clamoring of man-selves for a more-self deemed better-self. (Which, often, men endeavor to give themselves by robbing size from one another.) The cry of true need will be light, not loud, will be breathed, not hurled; and it will be answered with the event that women have maintained future in themselves, against the asking-day.

By men's mere surrender of their part-good to Whole-Good — mere wanting of the Whole, instead of the part! — and women's mere moving in mind from a sense of First Things and Last Things to a sense of Last Things in which First Things and Last Things are one actuality . . . by the mystery of Being, which is a mystery because of men, and no-mystery because of women, we, human, shall arrive, all, at our full actuality in Being, and Being at its whole actuality in us. And the story of ourselves as men and women will then have been told; and the further telling will then be in a Henceforth dating from our having become ourselves finally, become human selves finally, each one spelling One, each communicating All from the vantage of a fidelity of one to All as One.

|54| Almost I fear to approach the completion of my telling what I think we have to tell. Try, who read, not to put aside the words of my finish as an end of the subject, and the subject with them. Some of what you have here read you will have already dispatched to the category of the Strange, that to which your concern does not reach, some cast into the category of the Familiar, with the things you feel you always knew. I should like to speak here as at a beginning rather than as at an ending, so that you will not hasten to think "I have done."

|55| My subject is all ourselves, the human reality. And my subject is All, and One, the reality of All, of which we are the exponents. And my subject is Then and Now, the Then whence came our Now — the Now of complete afterness, if we but knew it. And my subject is the spirit that works between Then and Now. And over and over

it is the remembrance of Before, when Being was not numbered. If my words have the intonations of importunate appeal to your ears, let this be with you neither against me nor for me. I do not urge you to take my say for yours; I propose that you seek in yourselves remembrance of the Before, and tell what you find, and believe your words. How can we altogether believe the say of others unless we can believe our own? Many have been the stories of Before that have been believed without the believers having anything to tell of their own. But you will wonder if it could be possible to go back that far in memory. Ought we not to know how it Once was, does not the spirit in us ask us to know? . . . It is easier to know this from ourselves than from the stars, or the things that are less than stars, or all that is less than life, or all life that is less than us. For all these things hang between Then and Now in partial indetermination and inexistence, while the entire span between Then and Now is contained in our being: we can see all the way back to Before within the bounds of our being, and learn of it as our Before — and tell of it as our Beginning. Such a story of Before is not only our due to ourselves but to All-Being, which becomes in our telling our treasure, guarded by our words — is no longer left unhoused while we waste words storing the lesser valuables of time in truth's shelter. To know ourselves in a Now that has for past everything between primal Then and final Then, all-succeeding it, and all-preserving it through us, each moment, such is our due to ourselves; for in this now we can live All, Always.

|56| If you find something to tell, tell it to your truest, though that make little to tell; the truer you speak, the

more you will know to tell. If your words have the intonations of religious self-persuasion to your ears, be not uneasy, either that you presume, or that you belie your rational sobriety. We have all in us something of the voice of the religions. It is the voice of our Fathers, in their part-commanding, part-beseeching, themselves, men, to find enough Good in themselves for their good: there is a certain carnal panting in the sound of it. We shall all come to speak with the pure human tone as we the more speak the story of ourselves and the story of Being as one story — as we the more have One Truth to tell.

|57| We hover round the fact of the religions — in which Truth was told in two halves, God, and Man, which did not make One, but half, and, again, half. The religions nursed the further memory of our foregoers with their stories; and we in our later numbers can hardly keep from flocking to drink at their fountains of remembrance, which promise, all, to quaffers, the knowledge of First Things. Were they to make one story of their separate stories — as, indeed, some now plot to do, seeing that each of itself is not enough any longer to stand the tests of disbelief — that story would have in it the flaw of divided purpose that was in all the stories: not wholly for Truth's sake were those stories told, not wholly that the thirst of the knowledge of First Things might be quenched, but in a measure that the pain men suffer in being half-selves, selves of a half-world, might be softened, that their thirst for self-belief be quenched, and they feel at whiles a comfort as of wholeness . . .

|58| The tarrying of women at those religious fountains of remembrance of First Things can be seen amiss. They looked more fondly than men at the waters, and they delighted more in their sparkling on bright days, and they wept over them when they ran dark on dark days. They tarried where the fountains were, and where there were no fountains. But they always used a continuous, ever-renewed, momentary patience: they have been a more faithful than resigned company. Long before men will cry for life-in-full, women will have understood in their beings' otherness to men that the half-life of men's creation could not last. They have never been entirely at home in that life. They have taken it much to heart, but little to mind; and so it has been with the stories of Being of the religions. Women have had their hearts engaged, and over-engaged. But their minds, freer, have gone much ahead, to wait at the horizon of time till all telling of half-stories of Being cease, and half-life itself, and the Occasion of the Whole begin.

|59| You will perhaps be wondering, who have come with me this far, if I expect you to anticipate a change in the world and in yourselves of a universal magnitude? When I speak of our telling the story of ourselves to one another, do I mean that as many as can shall make a book-story, as I here have done, for others' reading? Is this telling, then, to be done by some for all, even as it has always been with telling? I expect you only to know that there has been a change when there has been a change; and that you will know it not as either a change in yourselves or in the world, or as a change great or small, but only as the change of speaking to one another with a constant reason of confirming Being in one another. And I will expect that

all our speaking to one another, then, will be as a book of one continual making.

|60| But in the immediate days we walk on the edge of that state of human dividedness that is not in its sum human. A fear holds back the human population of these days, as if beyond the edge were an abyss. Beyond is the putting-together: beyond is where Being puts itself together in us. There is a shrinking from that as from death-of-self, yet no going back. And so — on the edge of this place of the Middle Things (which come between First Things and Last Things) — we . . . they . . . you . . . dance the dance of the self, in its ultimate monotony of infinite diversity. Here and there the dance gives way to a marching to a monotonous music celebrating some concatenation wrongly called unity . . . And there is no going back: the Past of us is used. The half-world of our half-progress towards full selfhood (self-being touched with the touch of One) is being consumed in the war of its contradictions. Its half-words, with their meanings both double and divided, are destroying one another; and all that we call one 'consent' is a chaos of spoken incommunication. There is nothing left to us but to be sufficient to one another in our human need to pay to Being the debt of ourselves, that will enrich it with its Oneness, restored. All else has proved itself false — the difference between the insufficient and the false fading as the insufficient fades. There is nothing left to us but to speak in the pure language of this need — to speak only truth.

|61| Let us look to one another for signs of recognition of more than our numbered lone identities of the hour. Let us forget the too-little that we immediately know of one

another; also, what we thought we have known of First Things from the imitations of the far memory to which we have so much misfitted our souls. Let us look across the little identities of self, and across the great identities of kind into which we have been mercifully thrown together by fate (mortally foretasting in them the common bread of One-Being, the sustenance of souls); and look with one another behind the ages and the aeons, to an all-preceding All existent only to itself, reality total, whatever it might become; and then look with one another beyond ourselves-now, less than sufficient to ourselves, to ourselves sufficient to the total reality, giving it our life to live. The look behind and the look beyond can be accomplished in the same moment, the moment of departure from the edge of insufficiency — which we while away in these instant years dancing the dance of the self, or marching the march of a spurious One created out of our great belittlement of ourselves, or talking the talk of people who multiply everything by nothing to be sure they make no mistake . . . May our Manyness become All-embracing. May we see in one another the All that was once All-One rebecome One.

|62| And look upon one another with the look of One. And speak to one another with a self in which the selfhood of One moves, lives . . . If we will but begin, we shall continue, and there will be no end . . . Should my names and descriptions of things not draw for you or you the circle of entirety, draw you or you that circle, as you know entirety; if each different circle contains all ourselves, an infinite coincidence of truth will ring us ever round . . . Now I leave off.

*　*　*

(Later, consideration of the vices stirs up afterthoughts. A dangerous suggestion, is it . . . ? — that in the knowledge of entirety there can be such differences among us as might make you or you, not recognizing entirety in my storying of it, want to try yourself at the total subject? What if you or you — or you — should be a creature swollen with yourself, overfed with dreams of prevailing in the art of catching the ears of others, and set about to tell differently for the triumph of difference, and not for truth's sake?)

(Among human beings there are true differences of understanding, come of their having spoken so little with one another as beings of the one life-story. By speaking out of their different story-sense of human-being to one another, the differers can learn their life-sameness, and the different understandings be loosed to join. But — yes — there are also false differences of understanding. There are inventors of difference, bent greedily on having their *own* to say — whose different understandings are made jealously, not made of understanding at all.)

(Those of false-different understanding who might press forward to have a part in the making of our truth, stealing the name of it for their inventions, could do nothing other than follow the trace of old falsity, drawing the false circles that turn back upon themselves half-way. There is nothing new of false truth to suffer from. It will be repeated to the extinction of its capability of seeming new, true; we shall suffer from it only to the extinction of our capacity for being deceived.)

(As the number mounts of circles drawn by us to encompass the Story of the Whole, and the words begin to come faster from the different telling-centers, a spell of concentricity — the out-spoken force of original One-being travelling between them — will be upon us; and other than true-telling, whether in mutual error of difference or in the evil of isolate purposed difference, will become impossible. There will be no where in which, no when at which, to tell other-than-true, and no one to tell it. We shall have arrived at our ultimate identities, selves that Agree. And none will be missing from the count of those: it will tally perfectly with ONE.)

PREFACE FOR A SECOND READING

The Telling extends in subject across tremendous questions of existence and destiny, but I do not claim that their whole substance is compressed within it. Nor do I deliver it as gospel, though it is for me a personal evangel in that it unites some main thought-experiences of my life-up-to-now into an immediate word-of-faith. My purpose is to remind us that there remain still to be told the fundamentals of our being, and that we are the natural tellers of them — each a natural teller of a story of which we and Everything, together, are the Subject, the story of ourselves and everything that touches on us, everything we touch on. To speak briefly the sense of what I try to remind us of: we are left, still, with all to tell one another. I offer a method of treating of the Subject in its simple nakedness as ours — not covered with the traditional discourse in which it has been jealously sheltered, nor displayed in shameless caricatures, such as those with which the intellectual bazaars are now overstocked.

The essence of the method I offer is the idea that the task of treating of the Subject is the task of each of us; and that, each being but one, the method must be proportioned to the one-being of each. The method is in the assumption by each of the task, which is the task of truth: to tell what we know of our being, of how we came to be, and why, and what we are, and what we have yet to be. By my idea, the task of truth is divided amongst us, to the number of us — however large truth's subject is, truth can be no more than the speaking of an exact self, a being exactly one (nor can it be less). We must grasp the Subject with the tongs of our individual littleness; take the measure of it with what we are. If we do not, it becomes Monster Fact to us, and dwarfs us into invisibility to ourselves — or assumes, as it did of old, the vaporous look of legend to our imagination, which then reaches with giant head into Emptyness, in doltish rapture.

In showing how one may move to try to tell one's all, I have avoided chaptered abundance, and spaced myself to what it seemed any person, speaking out of a single identity, might need for keeping an appointment with the Subject. For I wished not to distract others with my telling from keeping their own appointment with the Subject; and to find a common measure of telling.

* * *

The Telling can seem, by the temper of the reading-matter of the time, not of the time. The reading-matter of the time is a theatre in which the play's subject is an everything consisting of what remains after the hardest-to-fulfil of good desires are removed from the field of desire. Vice and virtue, good and evil, are exhibited on the written stage in all forms but their own, the costumes designed to put the moral eye at ease, of an ineloquent variety, making the characters, who speak the same, look the same. The show exhibits an everything lacking Everything — lacking everything with which the purely human desires are concerned. The audience is acquainted with the later and later and latest in a curtailed humanness, presented as humanness humanized. It is educated in an advanced art of simplifying the Difficult, by making meaning mean less — how, for instance, to reduce the clarity of 'clear', the beauty of 'beautiful', the wisdom of 'wise', the truth of 'true', to handier limits of sense. The contemporary reading-curriculum is aimed at the reducing of the human state itself to something easier.

I have not tried to come to any terms, in *The Telling*, with contemporary reading-matter fashions, or to seal it from contemporary assault in a fashion out of fashion, or to outwit fashion by going beyond it in fashion. I wrote *The Telling*, rather than as reading-matter, as an interruption in the reading way-of-things. And it would be an interruption in any time. It addresses the reader as a speaker, one whose gift of reading is but the gift of speaking acknowledging another's gift of speaking. In my speaking in it I call on readers to interrupt themselves as readers, and make its subject theirs — it being ours. I speak in consciousness of them as having speaking of their own to do; and no curtain drops at the finish.

* * *

Our Subject has suffered much from 'method'. Immense methods of treating of it have been used in the past, methodologies that have overwhelmed it. Now, those methodologies have grown weak, and the Subject itself seems gone. An era of concern with *subjects* succeeds the eras of the methodologies, in which each methodology claimed the Subject as its own. The Subject is now denied in subjects; or, at the least, it is cast to impersonal distances, as if it had ceased to be profitable. The custom of the era prescribes that we distribute ourselves among the subjects, and know ourselves, and Everything, in portions, according to the piecemeal knowledge of the subjects. It makes us shy of all effort to speak whole-truth, as if this were antique folly, and recommends part-truths to our sagacity as requiring no correction, only to be replaced by others.

I have diverged here from the way of the era with the Subject, and from the way of the past with it, which was to make method its master. I have put to a test a method seeming to me helpful for the attempt to venture into the sphere of consideration of the Subject as our personal sphere, the very sphere of our being. Should we succeed thus in occupying this sphere, we should be using our small, individual simplicity for the understanding of the great simplicity of all-that-is; and, in the understanding of that simplicity, we should find an understanding of our own; and know the truth of the Subject and the truth of ourselves as one truth.

The intimateness of this method I present does not allow the force of doctrine to what is said. But doctrine is another's speaking given to one's mouth for one's own speaking, another's thinking given to one's mind for one's own thinking. I do not mean to facilitate the speaking of doctrine by others any more than I have meant to be speaking it myself. Doctrine is spoken to the uncertainty of others, and adopted as belief in uncertainty. John Stuart Mill said that people tended to believe in doctrines only to the point to which it is usual to act on them; and they are, indeed, temporary conveniences. All doctrines eventually lose credit with the believers of them, being more thinking-speaking custom, things of a time, than *truth* — ever-immediate truth. Nothing can be truth enduringly except what issues from our speaking to one another as joint authorities on the Subject, occupants of it as our thinking sphere, the world of our total speaking.

*   *   *

Readers must find me abrupt in my taking up the Subject with them. There is no key to my performance in the general pattern of literary performance of the time, which seems a complete map of the unprecedented. I have chosen not to slow the pace of *The Telling* by weighting it with the history of itself. But *here*, pausing perhaps before returning to it to read again, readers may find a proper repose in talk of its history, given apart.

The Telling has, in specific fact, two histories, one belonging to the personal, 'ordinary' human, record, one to the collective, officially human, record. The terms of the first should be quickly recognizable. The second history will require some terms of general historical analysis.

The immediate, private, or inner, history of how I speak as I speak in this book is centered in the curiosity towards our human-being we all continually have. It is a confused curiosity. We look for surprise and variety in our daily encounter with the nature of our being as if it were weather-like: our curiosity towards our human-being imitates the curiosity of body we have towards the weather. But the nature of our being is not to be known as we know the weather, which is by the sense of the momentary. Weather is all change, while our being, in its human nature, is all constancy. Humanness, though belonging to many, does not vary. We are inconstant in it, and so can be curious towards it as if it were itself inconstant, weather-like. But it is to be known only by the sense of the constant. The endeavor to exercise this sense is part of the history of *The Telling*.

All, surely, are conscious of turning now and again from their preoccupation with themselves as travellers through the weather of the ever-disappearing days to preoccupation with themselves as selves that are, and are. And, surely, in this pausing to claim their humanness, they know themselves to be returning to where they were and are and will be, from moments spent in the clutch of change? . . . know themselves to be outlasting what is momentary in what is constant — though but for moments? The setting of my book's speaking is such a place of return. I have done what others have done: I have made visits to the human actualness of my being. And, prolonging them in little-by-little gained awareness of my right to make them (that they were not stolen visits!), I came often not to depart — and to speak as I speak in *The Telling*. This history which I have related is an appeal to readers to translate the obtrusive effect of my going straight-way to speak on our Subject into the naturalness of the Subject they themselves from time to time suddenly know.

In relating the outer history of *The Telling* I must speak further of the 'methodologies' I have described, those professional caretakers of the Subject. I shall call them, here, professions. Certain professions have made our Subject their special care, dedicated themselves to the knowing of our Everything. In this time, there is rampant revolt against patience with the Subject, which has more and more acquired the outmoded look; but the custodian professions have persisted, observing at least the forms of custodianship.

The custodian professions serve in principle a laity inexpert in concern with the Subject. As the offices of care of the Subject are performed more and more perfunctorily, the laity feel more and more liberated from the necessity of concern with it: the need of authority seems to wane. But human beings cannot shun concern with the Subject, which is concern with the nature of our being, without over-throwing the authority of their humanness. Some, indeed, have tried to make a personal profession of concern with it, seizing upon empty places in the old, provided wisdoms as upon seats of authority, and teaching what is not enough for their own instruction. No makeshift, random wisdoms can save us now from the new ignorance, the false freedom, in which the Subject is thrown aside, as to darkness all its own. Nor could any methodology reconstruct itself, to provide new professional advice on the Subject to a laity become at once doubtful of authority and of the Subject's long and solemnly advertised importance. It is, indeed, a homely Subject: there has never been natural room for professionals, with *this* subject — the peculiar understanding of it of some could never do service as the understanding of it of all. Nothing could now or ever save us from loss of the Subject and loss of ourselves in the loss of it but the recognition of it as the special care of each, the special care of us all.

One of the professions that appropriate to themselves the function of treating of the Subject differs from the others markedly in its disposition to the laity: this is, poetry. I practised this profession many, many years, in ardent desire to improve upon its difference from the other wisdom-professions. The fact of poetry accounts for much of the outer history of *The Telling* — as I shall explain.

Poetry has seemed the guardian angel of our words. Where other wisdom-professions function in the character of intermediate authorities dispensing the Subject to the laity (according to their varying notions of it and views of the laity), poetry, in theory at least, brings the laity and the Subject together; its professionals conceive of themselves as representing the laity, as dealing on their behalf with the Subject in quasi-lay terms. It is the most genial of the wisdom-professions, aiming ideally at the exercise of a sensitivity to the Everything on which human-being opens free of restraints of dogma, and at a mode of expression of it in which the spontaneous essence of humanness can have sure and eloquent utterance. But the ideal aim of poetry is thwarted by its nature as a profession. As such, it must claim and prove authority, for as such it is a social agency, reflecting, subscribing implicitly to, the congenital authoritarianism of human society: it must justify itself by showing ability to sustain a formalism of its own in the environment of society's basic formalism. The power poets evoke in themselves to function as representatives of the laity in their dealing with the Subject is drawn greatly more from the surety of poetry's status as a socially valid profession than from the inspiration of their ideal relationship with the laity — and much more than they acknowledge to themselves.

Poets live bedazzled by the ideal beauty of their professional rôle. The poetic way of treating of the Subject can seem blessed by the natural authority of us all — can seem to poets and laity a way chosen by human nature, not imposed upon it by a wisdom that separates itself from human nature to rule it. But poetry does not escape the ineradicable fault of the wisdom-professions. It, too, presupposes a silent laity! The virtue poetry has of conceiving of itself as the voice of the laity is lost in the professionalism of the voicing.

All institutions of authority must give proof not only of a basis in reason, but of a basis in power. To endure in human society they must both prove themselves socially relevant and demonstrate a social efficiency; and this requirement tends, necessarily, to overshadow the former, even because the authority exercised must be of an institutional character, and the ability to impose it therefore outranks in importance the question of its rational validity. Poetry no less than other institutions of authority has its power-using, authority-imposing, devices. They are obscured in its charms: indeed, the charms may be said to be the devices! How like perfection can seem the poetic way of telling of ourselves, speaking of our Everything, speaking into our Subject . . . Yet, in the close, the closer and closer, look, this perfection can be seen to be colored with the love of professional power — to be not all incandescent with love of the Subject as the universal ground of truth (where words are released from every arbitrary service).

The liberty of word that poetry confers is poetry's technique, not truth's. The speaking domestication of human beings in their Subject cannot be more than symbolically realized in poetry: the technique of poetry cannot be brought to a point of intensity at which the silent laity is *given* its universal speech. At poetry's extreme of expressive intensity only professionalism can triumph — not the Subject, not truth, not poetry's laity (supposedly elevated in poetry from the nether muteness of the lay condition). Late in my own poetic professionalism I renounced the satisfaction of poetic success in words. *The Telling* is descended from that renunciation. I speak in it at the common risks of language, where failure stalks in every word. In speaking that is under poetry's protection, failure is scared away until all's said; small felicities of utterance magnify themselves into a persuasive appearance of truth. This success of art poets ennoble to a significance of virtue; in words throbbing with virtuosity's purposefulness they see a moral glow. In their sincerity of taking pains to persuade themselves of the goodness of what they do, poets attract

66

sincerity. But the sincerity of the laity cannot dissolve the mistakenness of poets — it is itself mistaken. Poems can seem to the silent laity to fill the void of their non-speaking, to be their speaking on the Subject. To a poet the mere making of a poem can seem to solve the problem of truth, which in other wisdom-professions is acknowledged to be a toilsome one. But only a problem of art is solved in poetry. Art, whose honesty must work through artifice, cannot avoid cheating truth. Poetic art cheats truth to further and finer degrees than art of any other kind because the spoken word is its exclusive medium; the product, reaching minds at instant quickness, scarcely leaves time for questioning of its entitlement to welcome as truth-natured utterance — as the very actuality, truth natural.

When I abandoned the poet-position, I took up place in the lay-position. Authority, then, required transposition from the poetic to the lay region: it had to be looked for wherever personhood, from which comes the ability to say 'I', is. It is to be found, in that region, in all the crossing pathways in which mutual assurance in the authenticity of 'I' courses to and fro from one to another. Such avowing of our being by each of us in truth's unity of interlaced responsibleness, *The Telling* suggests.

* * *

Readers may have wondered over the style in which *The Telling* is written: how to characterize it? Some may tend to think it 'poetic'. As it is veritably so, it has slipped from my hold. But 'poetic' is a greedy classification — it will take whatever is put into it. I myself think the linguistic character of *The Telling* more accurately describable in terms of *diction* than in those of style. Diction I consider to be the actual substance of style; and style, to be a vague, figurative identification of — a literary name for — diction.

I view myself as having spoken to the page, in *The Telling*, not engaged in a kind of writing. I have aimed at a normal diction, a kind that could be described as developed, or expanded, normal, in distinction from the familiar varieties of normal — the formal normal, the informal normal, the static conventional normal, the unstable unconventional normal (the list is amplifiable). What I have aimed at is an ideal. It is not one of my private invention, but a linguistically ordained ideal, every degree of fulfilment of which is a degree of express fulfilment of the hope comprehended in being, in its comprehending us within it, as human. This ideal is the total potential of human utterance, which has no limit except the bounds of rational congruity that language sets for it — a wondrous-seeming potential, though natural, because still strange to our tongues; we may go anywhere within it, and outside of it there is only place for saying what is mad or wicked to say.

I did not approach the making of *The Telling* from a point of decision as to what its diction ought to be 'like'. I composed myself in the making of it to a stand of non-predilection in the choice of the individual word and of words in phrased combination. I endeavored not to let any sort of bias or carefreeness in verbal taste rule the deciding processes. Unaccustomed choices of words and patterns of word-combination are found mingled in it with accustomed falls of speech. Some of what is unaccustomed, seeming simple accidents, could be taken for new commonplaces; and it may have an effect, generally, of stylistic variableness, because of not being formed with a predetermined literary diction-policy. On the whole, I think, a sustained unity of diction has been achieved in it; this opinion is supported by my having found, in my scrutinizing it after it was finished, that it forbade nearly all attempts at modification — those of incidental character included — that I was moved to consider making. I could not claim the distinction for it of being a perfect example of just diction. I can in good linguistic conscience aver that I have come closer in it to purity of motivation in word-choice than in all previous efforts of mine to do well by, and with, words.

My husband, Schuyler B. Jackson, who read in *The Telling* with a steady frequency to the day of his 'death', July 4th, 1968 (I write *death* so because he *is*, death notwithstanding, in the life-world of being I know), and whose knowledge and critical perception of the intrinsic qualities and proprieties of English diction are unexcelled, in my experience, communicated to me after long acquaintance with it that he held it to come nearer to the mark of the linguistic good than anything else he had ever read. I reproduce this view here not in pride (though I rejoice in his love of the little work), but in the feeling that it may help readers to establish *linguistic* bearings towards *The Telling*. The values guiding my husband in his view do not pertain, narrowly, to possibilities in 'writing', but to the plain — the universal — human possibilities in word-use. Such values, rather than categorically literary values, fixed to literary preconceptions about style, are crucial ones for judging of this work. What does it show of possibilities of pressing the language-potential towards a larger perimeter of the reasonable — there being so much to say by each, so much to tell . . . all to tell?

I have explained how I conceived of myself as offering, in *The Telling*, a method of our speaking, each, our All. I have meant by 'method', in the practical sense, nothing other than a kind of diction — diction liberated from both literary exactions and the banal latitudes imposed by everyday 'good' usage (which spares citizens from the conspicuousness of attempting whole goodness of speech), and also from the false rewards of linguistic libertarianism. Behind the identity, for me, of method and diction is no mere loose alliance of mystical sentiment and verbal preciosity. I have been engaged, with my husband, for many years, in preparing a work on language in which the relation between the spiritual basis of language and the rational principles informing it is traced, and the operation of those principles explored in the patternings of word-meaning; the work's object is the demonstration of the dependence of good (in all the senses) diction on the use of words with attentive regard for their individual rational nature, and the general function of language as the articulation of our humanness. I wrote *The Telling*, thus, within the fortunate scope of the illumination that my husband's and my studies imparted to the problems of human expression, in their character as, essentially, problems of diction. (I can only now make personal allusion to our work; but I look to its completion, and eventual public availability.)

In all that has been said by human beings from the beginning of speaking, there has been a stopping-short — even where maturity seems to have been reached — in the exercise of reason; and there has always been a tendency in conceptions of the linguistic ideal to give reason something less than a leading part in it. As I conceive the linguistic ideal, reason is not a median skill in the use of words but the ability to employ in thought the universal reference-points language establishes for the attainment of the human utmost: the human utmost is marked out in a linguistic utmost. And the unattained human-linguistic utmost I see as attainable only as a general end, by a general coming-of-age in reason. All this is in my principle of diction — and in the method of treating of our Subject that I offer. I have aimed at no special personal accomplishment. We have language, all, as a gift from one another for going apace with one another in advancing into our Subject: diction (or 'style') must be concerned, fundamentally, with our need of speaking to one another the ultimate confidences, in the exchange of which, only, do we know, and can we be, all we as human are — by the ultimate meaning of the word 'human'.

In the text proper of *The Telling* I am preoccupied with problems that can be drawn within the practical range of the solutions of diction. In these comments I am preoccupied, rather, with a general question *The Telling* must raise for readers: what to do because of it, with it, about it. I am, in these comments, that is, sharing in the common predicament of all of being uncomfortable in the idea or prospect of our standing inside ourselves, and speaking from there — we feel a safety in existing at removes from our human nature, not bound close to its verity. The diction of these comments is therefore divided between my sense of the possibilities, in our speaking, of exact human utterance and my sense of the obstacles we put between us and that: my attention is divided between the ideal, as the realizable, and the unideal, as the commonly preferred actual. I try to traverse the gap between the two, to show it to be traversable *in reality* — and with increase in safety, and sanity. There is more stumbling in my words, in these comments than in those of *The Telling* itself. But how should that not be? — since in these I do not begin my speaking on the far side.

*   *   *

As I formed *The Telling*, I kept excluded everything not belonging to it as primary substance; I planned to put the accumulating excluded matter-in-hand and matter-in-mind in an appendix. This preface is a very long after-piece, by the measure of *The Telling* itself, but the planned appendix would have been greatly longer. I decided to forgo the supplying of a massive supplement, wishing not to keep the work too long to myself. But there came a call to linger with readers, when I had finished, and begun to see them present to it, in anticipation. I found much to say to them in discursive critical comment — and, as I have proceeded, it has seemed increasingly important to me to take care to say enough. For, so far as I can foresee, from what is immediately available to readers in the reading-matter of the time of possible use in reading-difficulties they might experience with *The Telling*, they will have nothing to consult except what I can provide, supplementarily.

The planned sequel to *The Telling* was to deal with textually important matters of word-use, the meaning of portions of the text useful elaboration on which I thought could be made, the relation between some of the thinking peculiar to the work and that to be found in earlier writing of mine, the differences between the thought of past and present writers on themes of which I treat in the work, and my own thought on them. (I am aware of a likelihood of resemblances-seeing between the thought of *The Telling* and that of some philosophers. But my thought differs in the whole from that of any other contributor to the record of human thinking. Moreover, it is not characteristically philosophical thought: philosophical thought is of the nature of argumentation. I am not concerned with argumentation, but with *speaking*, with the speaking of all on our Subject, not with the philosophic matching of intellects.) I do not dismiss my sense of a need of further supplementary comment by me: I suspend it. *

*   *   *

There is a new silence on our Subject among us, now, an evilly all-pervading silence disguised in talk multifarious, touching on many subjects — talk in which desperate attempt is made to make this great not-speaking seem speaking. Should any speak now on our Subject, they would be at first unheard — or those who heard would be in difficulty, at first, to know what they heard. How many can have yet tried to speak on our Subject, or to hear speaking on it — how many know the evil of inattention to it, which destroys the human genius (that must be used for speaking all, or become itself nothing)?

There is no force in *The Telling* to work a magic of trans-

* A sequel of a sort will be seen to be, after all, provided; it is, however, not massive — and personal in mood, unofficial, as it were. — L.J.

formation in those prating away their human genius in talk on this-and-that in subject-vogue (none of it touching on the entire human subject, eternal). But, as I have explained, I see in it a method of our beginning to speak as ourselves, a way each might try for beginning the transformation from being one of the stranger-others we are for one another into being one of ourselves. There may seem a taint of spiritual condescension in this view of it. *The Telling* was written in my and my husband's faith in the sameness of the potential of perfection of being inhering in human nature with the potential of perfection of word inhering in language, and without any presumption of favoredness in either respect. In personal quality it is an act of love of ourselves, all, as human. I am resigned to letting it take, as such, the chances of love with others. Who reads condescension in my view of *The Telling* misreads its import of love.

The thought of others can thread its way soon out of range of the sense of the individual identity of each, and get lost. But if the sense of the single human identity of us all takes hold of the thread of thought of others, it cannot get lost. Thus, we can know people as nations: as nations, they are not merely unidentifiable others, but have an identity as portions of ourselves emblematic of the whole — the individual members of each being, indeed, gathered up into an 'ourselves' that breathes with a particular universality of united being. Because of the language in which *The Telling* is written, I am first conscious, in thinking of its general fate with others, of the English and the Americans: what of them as readers of it, what of them in relation to the comprehensive 'ourselves' to which it is addressed?

It can seem more difficult to characterize the national personality of the Americans than that of the English, it being a loosely assembled one, and that of the English a compact entity. This difference tends to make the English seem of a more serious nature, generally, seem, indeed, to promise more

universalness of human attitude; and the Americans to seem
more preoccupied with the fun of human existence, and their
own particular brand of that. Further, if one looks at the
English through the magnifying-glass of one's appreciation of
the virtues of their language, as I have, one finds them
impressive by reason of its nobility. But, if one looks at the
Americans through the magnifying-glass of one's American
birth, as I have, and knows the English language also as one's
own, its virtues gradually acquire in one's eyes a broad human
history — their English history seen as related to the sieve of
local circumstance through which they have been strained. All
who speak this language partake of an inheritance in which the
human potential and words' truth-potential have knit together: less than any other is it a vehicle of national peculiarities, special prides of a people. I cannot, in fact, envisage what
The Telling might differently be for American readers and
English readers with the help of linguistic clues; there are some
minor ones, but the actual difference between the Americans
and the English is not a minor one.

I see Americans as having had fall to them a responsibility
never assumed by any before them as one requiring unequi-
vocal fulfilment: it is, to define human nature. All human
beings before the Americans have, in their varied grouped
representations of humanity, dealt with the responsibility in
metaphor, till the reality seemed little more than a loose
indispensable supposition, mortal subject of mortal thought.
"Discover what human nature uniquely is!" immortal
humanity asked, in the West. The Americans found a first
answer: to thrive beyond all known thriving, exceeding ever
the last limit. But the attained was ever by definition, thus,
disproved. Disliking failure, they have tried to make a happiness of restiveness, and to lose self-dissatisfaction in the
unreproach of others; or — and this increasingly — to play
doubt and faith against each other, unhappiness and happiness,
hoping to gain time for wisdom's coming. And all the while the

faithless World catches up with them in human time. And they are unready.

As those completing the human circling of the earth, making a world of it, the Americans have no historical threshold to cross into final self-consciousness in the human rôle. They are no steps away from the state of being ourselves in being themselves. As a journey's final lap can verify the intent of what went before, so could they refer a full mindfulness of human destination to the earlier portents — work the features of ultimate human meaning into the vague human countenance of the past. Nothing hinders them except that what has fallen to them to do has never yet been done: suppose their defining of human nature displeases others? They must so define it that there are no others to please or displease; the literal definition of human nature will bring all within the community of their identity as ourselves. For this problem of delayed courage, of the Americans, in which their desire for their own happiness keeps overflowing aimlessly with desire for that of others, *The Telling* might provide at least some of the terms of spontaneity.

The English I see as having had given to them by fortune a rôle of defining the good. They have nurtured a persuasion of loving the good on the tested moral discoveries of the past, as they have nurtured a persuasion of loving truth on word-treasure cast up on their national shore. Nobility rather than human nature is their spiritual specialty. I have lived and worked among them, and honored them in the high rôle of their adoption. There is a largeness in their consciousness of the World; but island-appetites have ruled in it — in their attachment to the World they kept ever on the self-regarding side of attachment. Unlovelinesses of self-love dapple the noble appearance, unchangingly. Nothing will change, there, without a certain self-forgetfulness. If I could but, with *The Telling*, distract them a while from their mirror! Their need is, to have their born condition of heart reverse itself, so that, beginning again, they start in the love of others. Loving others, this could indeed be a people to teach others the lessons of good.

But, truly, I am not curious as to the likelihoods and unlikelihoods of *The Telling*'s having a place in the counsels of others concerning their humanness. For there can be no special knowing where it has had success with others, since the success will be success of them, not it, and the credit of that would be theirs. Nor did I, in making it, face myself and it towards this quarter, and that quarter, though I am sensitive to the differences between people, in their different quarters. I faced myself round, I faced it round — without preferences or prejudgements. Who would be included in its intention is included; who would not be, is not.

* * *

To speak of ourselves as beings of our time. — Our time seems to teach us that we are the stuff out of which all that we can be must be made. But the lesson omits the endeavor dwelling in us to reach a full, a final, humanness — the endeavor that gives sight of the possible. We think of ourselves, now, only as rubber, stretchable somewhat. In other times, where we have guessed that we fell short in gathering-in, entire, the substance of human-being, we have committed ourselves again and again to the guardian-angelship of the endeavor (our most truthful teacher to us of what-we-may-be and what-we-are-not). This indefatigability has been a saving virtue, in failure.

Our time that teaches us, now, a sophisticated weariness of ourselves, human with difficulty, is a false time. Our real time is of the time-succession that is the World's time, the recorder of all incompletion and completion, all failure and success, in being's faithfulness to itself: the total account awaiting the total information. The false time is a prophet to our own niggardliness towards ourselves as human, vouchsafing to us a human Further that will cost us nothing of effortful difference from what we have been.

I have tried, in *The Telling*, to speak hearing the unbroken rhythm of the World's time, and feeling in my words the accents of an immediacy intuitively comprehensive of the yet not wholly experienced whole of Event. I present as our real time a now that has all that has made, and makes, Event, and will make it, in human view — that exposes to us, for learning, the entirety of our being. I reject the false human news that a false time now publishes about us, according to which we are graduating into a new mortality, in which we can live, while insisting on our mortalness, *as if* we were immortals. I disbelieve in this as a pious diabolism; it is a deadly perjury pouring ventriloqually from the hell of human self-weariness, seeming, falsely, to issue from the real mouth of the time, to speak with the actual voice of the time itself. I evoke in *The Telling* an immediacy free from those prejudices against ourselves that have escaped from our history and make themselves at home in our time as if we were not there — an immediacy in which, befriending the fact of us, we begin to comprehend the reasons of the fact, and rejoice in having more to be.

* * *

Question of the temporal relevance of a writing brings with it a trail of literary considerations. I present now, finally, a view of the literary background of the time, against which some readers of *The Telling* will undoubtedly try to set it. First, I quote some words of T. S. Eliot's expressing a conception of literary modernism that still colors contemporary literary thinking. Speaking in praise of what he called 'the mythical method of modern writing', he declared it to be "a step forward towards the making of the modern world possible for art". And he defined the modern world as an "immense panorama of futility and anarchy". I too have talked of 'method'. But my method is for the treating of a Subject from the reality of which our own is inseparable, and for the treating of it by us as ourselves-in-the-World in this time of the World's time — taken by me to throb with our own pent expectations of us, insisting themselves. Eliot's method is fashioned in mockery of these expectations, even in denial of our having a real Subject: it is a mock-method for the treating of a mock-Subject.

The mythical view of ourselves did not fall away entirely *until* this time. That is why we have had so much of prayer for new myth sent up from the literary altars: there seemed to be, the mythical view fallen away, nothing to write about! . . . And why we have had so much invoking of the sense of myth for the utterances put out with the label 'modern': their sense was thinner than that of myth! We had just begun to emerge from the obscurity of the mythical view of ourselves when the literary priesthood took fright at the prospect of having to confront the actuality of human existence at first hand, without any intervening ritual of verbal incense-burning and mystery-making. A new literary magic was devised, that reduced the actuality to a fact of pathos and absurdity (held in meaningless balance) while reinflating the old myth-propensities of the human mind with improvisations of pseudo-myth — art taking over where imagination had departed. *This* was modernism. The spell of pseudo-myth it cast fogged the real modern intelligence, blotched the real look of the World, and of ourselves within it: what is there to see by the real light, in the real air, of the time has been hardly seen.

The mist of modern pseudo-myth drizzled down pseudo-disillusionment. Eliot's identification of 'the modern world' as an immense panorama of futility and anarchy has plausibility only in a literary scene arbitrarily equated with the natural time-scene. But the pall of pseudo-mythical notioning that settled over the literary scene spread in loose floatings far out from it; and to that pall-making Eliot himself contributed a not inconsiderable production of cloud. Others have contributed to the modern literary fume, many in larger volume, and some perhaps with greater morbific effect. I single out Eliot because he made himself literary modernism's official arbiter, introducing into it standards of respectability appropriated from the literary past, for its dignification: he was more responsible than any other for the supine acceptance by the time, as an authentic spiritual emanation of itself, of a literature of miasmic unseriousness and disloyal irrelevance to the time's human age.

Neither myth nor pseudo-myth has true place in our time-scene. We have need of all the life-space they have taken up for the effort to be all that the human image has foreshown of humanness. Myth gave ignorance consoling companionship. Pseudo-myth could only attend us in pseudo-ministration — a 'culture' manufactured to surround us with the comforts of confusion. The culture, the 'modern world', the futility and anarchy, the time, ourselves, became indistinguishable; all being confused, confusion itself ceases to be recognizable. New possibilities, not only for art but for hitherto unthinkable forms of untruth, strew the literary scene — become indistinguishable from the time-scene; present and future blend in an ever-expanding immediacy of deterioration in immediacy of hope. This process has seemed to prosper into a collective human self-understanding, to which has been given the name 'compassion'. But it is a cruel elevation of pitiableness to admirableness, in which we hope for less, less, for one-another-all, to a degree of hopefulness so close to hopelessness that we do not hope — we have 'compassion'. And writers multiply, hoping less, less, telling less, less, in larger, larger, voices. The people fête upon banquets of commiseration with their 'condition' (of being human — as pure, essentially unalterable injustice), and ask for more, more.

Such is the modern literary background of our personal modernity. It is an imprisonment. Our vision, drawn into it, beats against its dank light. In the past I have tried to shine light into it, and out of it, thinking that the fit speaking of the time might begin there, in a brightness of literature exceeding the mere literary limit of the possible in words. I placed myself in *The Telling* in a scene in which the human implications of contemporary literary modernity can show only as the detritus of a false temporal horizon. *The Telling* is set in the open. What open? I believe we are here in the modern open, Readers.

October 2, 1968

SOME AFTER-SPEAKING:
PRIVATE WORDS

AN INVITATION

I call what I am writing here 'private words' because they are not spoken, as are the words of *The Telling* proper, by myself, one, to each other one as belonging with me in human unity of kind (myself as belonging so with them) to truth, and having a potential of true-telling both awesome and natural. *These* words are spoken from the midst of our differences, by myself in separation from every other. I am, that is, the author retired from the open of public address to the afterwards of her private thoughts. And everyone who reads here will be reading in a private capacity, rather than in the public capacity of a member of the book's audience, as it is with the text of *The Telling*, and, even, the Preface — which has been brought to the text's rear as marginal to it, not so much a way into the auditorium of its sense as a way *back* into its auditorium, for hearing again, with promptings for ears that want to hear better. The delivery, and the hearing, are over! The forces of common-occasion have been disbanded. I am not speaking *out* here to a summoned collective YOU. A *you* or *you* of voluntary chance comes *in* here to browse my after-thoughts, made available, rather than by the insistences of authorial invitation, by the hospitality of my private conscience.

I imagine some, at least, who have read in *The Telling* to a point of believing that I *mean* it, thinking: "What comes next? What does this imply as to what might, could, or should follow?" For such there would be a troubledness, as when next pages are blank: 'where is the rest of the story?' I myself know a troubledness as to 'what comes next'. But I know also a patience of meaning what I have spoken that enables me to rest at it for as long as 'next' is not yet, or has not yet dis-

tinguished itself from what is and was, in time's confusion of
times. For, as long as next is not tellable with truth's immediacy, as that which has distinctly succeeded, these after-
pieces will, I think, fill the blank of arrested expectancy for me
for so long, and so long; and in such transient composure I, and
those who, having read, wait for More, as do I who have
written, can learn to suffer better in our being's incompletion,
and rejoice better when what comes next comes, and we fulfil
ourselves in time's explicit fullness.

I have told, in the Preface, how I abandoned an intention of
incorporating with *The Telling* a complex exercise in textual
scholarship. Some of the matter I had accumulated for this
is represented in this Part. But what is offered here is different
in purpose, and considerably different in content, from what I
had first intended. *The Telling* has for many months, for
several years, indeed, lain unpublished (as a book, that is);
however, my reasons for abandoning my intention to provide
an elaborate supplement hold good still. *The Telling* was —
and is — spiritually a finality. What follows is not meant to
labor the matter of finality but only to provide an interim area
in which readers may try the work's future durability, if they
wish, retiring there to expend impatiences excited by it —
impatiences with time, *The Telling* itself, myself the author —
in patience with themselves. Such is the character, for me, of
this Part.

2

THE IDEA OF REBEGINNINGS

It was in the days immediately following that on which my husband Schuyler died (July 4th, 1968) that the idea of Rebeginnings took form in my thoughts. I was conscious, then, of all that does not change, as this is perceptible from the personal viewing-point in the acute light generated by a briefly tremendous moment of change-violence. But what I saw as the same, still, in my husband's and my being — as uninterrupted conjoining of being — consisted not of Old Things, the substance of past time mortuarily perpetuated, but of New Things, Rebeginnings made to turn the course of being away from the misturns that age it away from its due direction, which is, towards an expressed completeness. This will seem a boast: that *we* were not, are not, as others, that *we* took the right turnings towards that 'due direction' of the course of being, and so are now safe, in our special fashion, from being consumed by time — that *we* moved, move, with it. Oh, there could be no boasting, in this condition of ours. There can be no stop in the moving, to say " *This* is the Complete!" Such a boast would prove only a coming to rest at the end of a misturn, and be not an expressed completeness of being, but a cessation commemorating itself with a lie — a lie that makes nothing final except mortality.

I am speaking here *along the way*, only. And I mean that way in which the steps become more and more Rebeginnings, until all has the freshness of Beginning; — until all going on is without misturn, is New, with, yet, the finality of expressed completeness attained, continuously and unrepetitively, as it could only be. Who could make boast of thus going on, in being, along this way — of belonging more and more to the expressing of being, the whole expressing of its whole? Along this way there is no air in which self-congratulation could breathe. The Expressing claims all air, all that we are and exist by . . . I leave this question of boasting, which raises, suddenly, what is not to be made briefly understandable.

My husband had the touch of spirit for making Rebeginnings, and pursuing the promise of each to — at the least — the justification-point, where the promise proves itself worthy of the pursuit, though no actuality fill grasp of knowledge. All he did had the mark on it of the courage to look into the further, the far, and not draw finish-lines where vision reached mere temporal bounds of vision. To be thus is to be of the forever-quick. Such renew the course of being in themselves, and (I am sure!) are renewed in it, beyond the range of bodily time, of the sightings from here to there.

The difference between those who aim at a finish, at finishings, and those for whom completion is endeavor's aim cuts through many areas of human activity. The concern with 'finishing' can produce successes that lack true finality, have too restricted a field of reference to apply usefully to general human circumstance, though attaining the status 'important' in the locale of their appearance. These successes can be books-by-themselves, movements in literature and the products of these; works of art of their own exclusive identity, or movements in the arts and the products of these; trends in philosophical, religious, political, scientific thinking and the manifestations of these. The forms that the preoccupation with making a finish takes are so many that it would be difficult to fix upon a single one as markedly illustrative of it. But the single word 'finishers' serves for the persons acting by these various forms — who draw others (those who merely read, watch, wonder what to approve) into the currents of their achievements, according to the success of these as seemingly shortening the difficult course of being. Fatal simplifications!

Yet of such, mainly, the history of human success consists. Overshadowed by that history is the story of how it has been with us in our past, and into our present up to yesterday, as to the endeavor to move in the direction in which only there is no end that is not completion of knowing being — and that no end, except that false accounts, skimped descriptions of the being of us, work of the impatience-to-be-done, shall have then become impossible. What has, truly, been achieved in progress towards fullness of knowing being is obscured by the works of the 'finishers', which crowd the historical horizon — so that there is no just seeing to where, by truth's measurements, we have come, no just seeing where we are, in our advance as beings charged with carrying the spirit distributed in us to a point of union, of us in it, it in us.

In these times in which the word 'revolution' is freely used to dignify, or, else, denounce, the continual commotions shattering social peace in many lands, communities, vicinities, a close look at the implications of the word would yield a better understanding of the commotions. Revolution solemnly conceived has rebeginning as its — at least — ideal objective: it is theoretically — at least — aimed at, if not practically, immediately, concerned with, fundamental differences in the future course. The commotions current in these times are programmatically defined in the verbiage of bold ideologies, but they are only loosely so defined, and only to dignify impulsive intransigence. This is why there is so much pastiche of Marxism, Mao-ism, Zenism, Mohammedanism, guitar-strum or band-beat, so much describing of things complex with simplicity, as they hardly are, so much facile psychological, sociological, anthropological, pedantry in the intellectual background of contemporary commotion-making. Mere cessation-making, not revolutionary projection futurewards from present conditions judged unfavorable to the human good and happy, is the objective of the present-day commotion-makers:

87

they want to 'get it all over with', be finished with responsibilities of concern with the beyond-today. Professional revolutionaryism, historic liberalism, typical modern radicalism, have all become assimilated to the feeble intellectual motivation that characterizes the agitated contemporary pursuit of change — and assimilated to one another, in their adapting themselves to its emotional mood, which is anti-visionary, not visionary. To progress towards an ambitiously conceived desideratum is not the concern of the 'advanced' opinion of the time: it is to call a halt in idealistic aspiration and come to rest at low-level, limited-objective alternatives to it. It is conservatism, now, that is the intellectually official defender of idealism!

The passions of dissidence of the present that seem of revolutionary heat are fretful rather than ardent. Indolence and short-temperedness mix in them. Hope has been replaced with a pattern of haughty demands made of fate for what are but pittances. Hope needs the food of generous courage. These who cry out now, asking for surcease of all that requires dedication of themselves to the future of all, and for the bestowal of their full and final share of the human inheritance upon their *now*, an immediate distribution of the common human wealth, have trimmed away the generosities of courage in themselves, and make bold with miserly demonstrations of it, that commit them to nothing beyond this crying-out for their share, and a quick reply. The substance and quantity of the human wealth is not calculable in terms of greedy individual or collective appetites for it. It is not thus divisible, or, in this manner of reckoning, knowable. It is knowable only by those who, making themselves part of it, proceed and proceed to learn and learn its magnitude, which is that of Being comprehending the beings who go on and on loyally to the infinite point of completion, with themselves, of Being's story — and, thus, to ever-intimate and entire acquaintance with 'how much' there is of common wealth.

The issue is not between those who clamor for a settlement of accounts with them, by fate, *now* (whose libertarian theatrics win for them an unearned reputation for — even religious! — earnestness, among those who have lost their human sense of direction and look blindly about for something to call 'Next') and the surviving idealists girded with sagacities of caution against the false appeals of the falsely new. These contestants have their backs to each other. The clamorers, of course, award themselves a continual victory of not being countered with a loudness as outcrying as their own. But there are no voices calling from a higher ground of human vision, in tones bespeaking exhilarating sight seen, "Come, look!" The decryers of Hope — and decryers of humanity in this, for what has humanity been, in its keeping on being itself amidst so much uncertainty of self, except Hope — lay out a new human scene that is aseptically hopeless. The foundation-premise of their different world is, there is nothing to go on from, nothing has yet been *gained*: let us have our due, let the rewards of fortune that humanity has been laboring so long to deserve be distributed. And what does each, then, get? Each can thus get only each's self! And the substance of the human treasure, thus divided up, vanishes: into the poverty of each. For the self of each, in itself, is a poverty.

Some American negroes have added a primitively nihilistic sentiment to the clamor-philosophy that has become part of its sophistication for the light-faced followers of it: they reject the American-and-'Western' experiment in human progress as a ruin, largely because it has been slow in making happiness for negroes forcibly brought into the sphere of it (who, actually, managed to make some for themselves, under far greater difficulties than those under which they now live), pronouncing negro rejection of it to be delivery from it for all. To the light-faced clamorers and the light-faced ones who opinionate in unison with them, the sentiment is a bitter pill welcome as morale-medicine.

Light-faced and dark-faced ones, in their varyingly angry activities of attempting to identify finality with the lack of vision of a next that is not mere dust kicked up from what lies underfoot, conceive of themselves as heroic initiators of a state of human existence facing a new outlook. And an admiring audience, older heads, wary of the burden of being the wiser, accepts this curtailment of the labor of vision hurriedly, just when what lies directly beyond calls for a final purification of sight (how many ways, now, of shrinking from this call, which none can escape feeling, somehow . . . !) and applauds the commotion-making as new life breathed into the body human. And boos and hisses at the body politic that would outlaw total outlawry offering itself as a gift of total redemption to society. And the body politic is driven to shame-faced uncertainty as to where the body human is, of which it is the outer protector, from which it must get its orders of heart and mind. It is not in what has been named 'the liberated zone', where that outlawry camps in an inhuman domesticity of disorder-tolerant-of-itself. Nor is it in the keeping of those who believe that Sobriety, providence-like, will in its own good time fill what has been left blank in the still uncompleted human miracle, under the name of the future. Or, in the keeping of the hand-clapping intellects who put their faith in the clamorers' no-faith — as if this spared them the old responsibility of choosing a true, a right, faith and all risk of believing false, being wrong.

Who among us knows anything? Another way of framing the question is, Between whom and whom does the issue lie? But who recognizes the issue? The argument is taking place at the wrong scene, with all the contestants acting in the wrong capacity. And it is the wrong argument. And I could as well say, they are the wrong people! — : they are people gone straying at the point at which all further straying takes *out of* the terrain of possible errantry in travelling the human course of being, with perhaps just a few feet, if as much, of retraction-room left before the falling-off edge, where the reason of human identity plunges into the abyss of Waste. (They being then but babblers arguing themes humanly meaningless to them themselves — meaning to them only opportunities to sound humanly alive in their own ears, to the degree of their bodily-pride's desire for self-witness.) And *that* is the issue: the reason of human identity. And there is no argument possible about it except between those who, turning and turning away from every angle of short-work making, or shorter, of being human, are in a contest of loyalty to the identity, and of joy in rebeginning, as far and far as is needed for Being to regain a final full, in its journey in us to explicitness — to a freshness such as Beginning has. It is a contest of joy in one another. The watch for 'Who?' is a watch for who-can-take-perfect-joy-in-one-another. In the final state of acquaintance with one another there are no other 'who'.

Human beings have moved much, in their onwardness, in cycles of repetition, in which nothing is confirmed but that there was an eventual creation of beings within a primary creation of number athwart the single actuality, Being. The primary creation was for proof of Being to Being: it was the putting out, into being, of the material for the complete analysis of Being, and testing of its integrity. And the creation of beings within this experiment within which certitude was made the judge of itself was for the speaking of the presence of Being in being, so that all that is might have express belonging in all that is — so that knowledge of Being might permeate being through beings in whom would gather and from whom go out the tidings of the unlosable unity of all that is.

But if those beings, eventual beings possessed, in inward intimateness (after much labor, Being's laborings of creation, for distinction between selves, *speakers*, and mere number, — mere, varyingly, bemused or possessive recipiency of existence), of knowledge of Being in the form of sense of self, betray the entrustment to them of such telling? And make it the reason of their humanness to insist repetitively that they are, *to* Being, as to an audience present to them in continuous repetition? *This* is 'the Fall'! — known in sinuosities of avoided awareness, by that legendary name, to man's conscience, as an archaic tradition, a moral invention. But the betrayal *is*, the duty to Being is ignored, intelligence is used for denying knowledge of it: theft of being has been greatly the human employment, disguised as the mere course of human nature. Human nature is a secret for our making open; it is a self-being, selves-being, on Being's account. The fulfilment of this nature is not in becoming talking curiosities of live individuality in the universe, able to boast newnesses in modes of self-being, the human secret but an infinite variation of the abstract personality of change. All that we are, human, is ultimately uneventful repetition of the creation of beings, ultimate count of nothing's having happened, of our being, *except* as our selves are Being rebeginning in us in new all-specific being-one, through a peopledom of our selves given to our nature's uses, not kept for our own.

We — are we not all the same 'we' in that we have for ours to take to a right destination the course of being we call 'human'? — have been too much at ease in our human state, in our assumption of it as a completed effect. We have used the creation by which we are as a fortuity, given it its end in ourselves, instead of letting our beings travel the difficult onward course for which they are fitted by their creation. How can we not think, from our being possessed of capabilities for which the *difficult* has no meaning of impossibility, that we have not a more difficult task of being than to fill our existence with that of existence which will justify our existence to ourselves? Our task of being is to restore Being to wholeness in ourselves yielding up the little whole of self we are, and are, to piece Being . . . To repair the very dispartment of Being in creation *with* being, our being, our beings. Such is rebeginning; such is the further course of our being as new course, the course of the correction of creation's errors, accidents, failures, incompletions — in ourselves.

But what I am saying I mean to have the sense of what each one may comprehend and do, of self's own comprehending, and doing; I mean it to have the sense of what each one may be, how be, from inward determination, not under a *plan*, by which some determine the means of salvation of human existence, the spiritual *policy* that all should follow to be human beings rightly. Who, alarmed in these times, look for such a plan, pine for such a policy, are in their fearful weaknesses invokers of foolish prescriptions for the cure of world's ills by those who have the false strength of ignorant daring. (Thus have the young, distraught from being taught less and less, been envisaged by distraught elders, teaching less and less, as perhaps the destined devisers of a new spiritual government for the world.) What I have been saying I mean to have effect only personally — if it has effect; indeed, it could have effect only so. It is for each to find or not find good what I have been saying; and even if it is found good, the judgement itself must be put under judgement. The general consequences, in this way of treating of our troubles of humanness, could be unhappily slow in developing: the effect might seem motionless. But there might be particular happily fast-developing consequences, in one, and another, or another. And that would be a beginning — a true trial of what I have described as rebeginning.

I spoke, parenthetically, a few sentences back of how the young are distraught, from being taught less and less. The pity of it is not merely in their ignorance but in the growing persuasion, in them, and their elders, of there being a *basic* nothing-to-know. From this comes the trend towards enthusiasm for the freedom of irrationality. If the orientation-points of knowledge fade, and every mark on the map of intelligence is a zero, not subject to increment, then every direction, every goal, is as good, and bad, as another; and human existence itself is a Zero, 'structured', to use the here apt jargon-word of the contemporary philosophic higher ignorance, to rise to a top of self-understanding exactly like the understand-nothing bottom. What happens to the teaching-tradition in this 'cultural' atmosphere has an aspect of horror — the dissolution of the identity of desirer-of-instruction and of that of provider-of-instruction in a common beginning-and-end point of know-nothingness, on which is bestowed a psychological value of know-everythingness, and an aspect of pathos. The latter shows in the head-scratching dismay of some of the teachers in the 'humanities' area of instruction over the difficulty of finding a *raison d'être* for teaching in the midst of the overwhelming accumulations of evidence of the potency of irrationalism provided by its latter-day products in literature, art, philosophy and social behavior. These survivors, honest enough to profess a hankering to *teach*, accept the dominating intellectual view of the time, which is, that knowledge — knowledge in the grand sense of knowing what we are and what all that is is 'all about' — is an irrational ideal, and yet cling to a vestigial teacher-consciousness in themselves that, were this so, the entire fact of our humanness would collapse, and, with it, the great heart of the subject-matter of teaching, that is, our progress as human beings in the progress of knowledge of ourselves as such. They are too much intimidated by the intellectual prestige that has built up around cultural exploits in the irrational to contest the authority of the exploits on the ground that they are irrational. *Who has established that what is irrational is right, and not wrong?*

A friend who values my thought, and what I say and tell in *The Telling*, and in connection with it, has wished for my pausing, here and there, to provide illustrative instances. So,

I shall pause here to quote from what a professor of English at Columbia University, Mr. Robert Gorham Davis, wrote in *The New York Times Book Review* (of June 28, 1970), in illustration of the condition of dismay of which I have spoken — dismay tinged with impotent longing for a way to resist that which is while deferring to it as irresistible. No more, he declares, can the teaching of literature be regarded as "a rational, objective discipline like the teaching of science".

A wealth of historical fact is available and an infinitude of brilliant insights. A tremendous articulateness has developed which fails, though, to articulate in the sense of uniting, of joining things together. Where interpretation and judgement are concerned, we teach only opinions, not knowledge. — Students are given case books with exactly opposite interpretations of [examples provided] ... Though literature has always been important to men, *we have no way of assessing its specific effects for good or evil.* [The italics are mine.]

What I have just quoted is a confession — coming from out the very seats of knowledge, the inner university-precinct of contemporary consciousness, which has the public charge not only of correcting the misknowledges of the past but of preserving the found knowledge of the past, and of enlarging this — of utter inacquaintance with any guide of judgement. The trunk of knowledge in the matter of good and evil that humanity has brought along in its journeying in the course of being has been emptied. And not only this: it has been thrown away, in accordance with the pluralistic enthusiasm of the time for the false freedom of total incertitude. And all who hold themselves to be knowing in that new-found not-knowing carry a pack upon the back especially made with holes to let what is put in fall out. These proclaim the empty pack to be the symbol of their yearning for unity in the midst of their celebration, which they call 'existential', of the satisfactions of existing by a theory of mass-separatism according to which the reality of existing is the continual falling-apart of

95

the separatist-mass — one's 'identity' conceived to be in the perfect identification of oneself with the flying fragment, oneself, as it goes its way to the unity of dissolution.

I have not yet dwelt, here, on that aspect of knowledge-activity in which it is, rather than a functioning in oneself of a service to one's human nature, a functioning in oneself of the human service to Being. This service is the using of the concentrative power of the intelligence to gather, from the seemingly illimitable plurality of things that are, the fact that Being *is* unity, and that this unity is the good. Every human being in being human has a private consciousness of such a something-to-be-done, such a knowledge-work due from the intelligence, a care to know for more than the satisfaction of the intelligence. Entwined in us with the will to be 'articulate' (to take the Professor's word) is a will to render Being articulate, in a knowing of its nature in which the intelligence works for *it*. [Thus, the eventual elimination of evil, as a perjuring against its nature!] There is no representation, in the public seats of knowledge, of this aspect of knowledge-activity, to save the day of knowledge (and, so, the day of teaching). The trails of divergence from the straight course of human being have been branched and diversified by the exuberance of scientific experiments in knowledge to the point of contemporary life's being overcast with a hypnotic influence that leads (almost) every mind off-course, as it were off-earth, into an all-directioned sophistication. The instinct of that crucial knowing (which is the crucial element of the human-being) is (almost) lost in (nearly) all of us. — And I speak here of 're-beginning'? When I see the Race in flight from itself, in a dispersion in which the course of being is not merely bent but broken-with, broken-away-from?

How is the way (the line of pre-knowledge that takes as always partly aright, leaving the rest to knowing's choice), when lost, to be found again? At what point in lostness of way can there be findability of way? Human beings are so made that even in the midst of ignorance and its errors they know of a difference *false* and *true*, by the inborn purpose of truth that makes the difference called human. They think of the false as their unlike, and, if they pay it the suicidal compliment of treating it as true, converting themselves into believers in it in order to prove it to be the true, they are still — loving the false as the true — within the reach of their own birth-gift of love-of-truth: there are still moments left for their calling themselves back to a rebeginning. Anywhere, anywhere, everywhere, everywhere, in a human being's being can be a point of rebeginning so long as the false is not loved *as the false*, because it is the false.

I have spoken of my husband Schuyler, as one who had the touch of spirit for making Rebeginnings, and pursuing the promise of each to — at the least — the justification-point where the promise proves itself worthy of the pursuit, though no actuality fill the grasp of knowledge. Shall I not record for who might read here my personal understanding, from knowing him and knowing his death, how there is no danger of disappearance from being — no danger of not living — where love of truth is of the very same press of being in us as life itself? — But are we companions in being knowing one another well enough to talk of one another to one another, or are we Members of Society at the distance from one another of Society?

It is mistaken to think that there has been in these times a revolutionary change from the institutional to the personal in action and expression. People are speaking to one another more loudly than ever as Members of Society, and less audibly than ever as companions in being. The change that appears to have been effected at the centers of higher education from the institutional to the personal approach in the treating of the subjects of human concern, in response to clamor of the studentry for such a change, is but the substitution of a purposefully disorganized institutionalism for one that had become

97

involuntarily lax. It is a change made in nervous pacification of an institutionalized criticism of institutionalism overflowed from present-day — torrential — political and social hostilities onto the extra-impressionable ground of a youth encouraged into precocity by exposure to an expansive scepticism indulged in over-sanguinely by the general adult part of Society.

I shall add to the example I have given of current academic attitudes to questions of knowledge, understanding, judgement, two others. The voicings of attitudes are in both cases those of professors at Princeton University, treated of in special articles in a 1970 issue of the *Princeton Alumni Weekly* as exemplars of 'a new humanism', editorial reference being made to pronouncements of Professor William Arrowsmith of the University of Texas on the difference between 'the formal humanism of the old university' and that of the contemporary university, to the latter being ascribed connection between its theory and its practice, to the former a concern with its theory only, causing it to lose 'its power as ethos'. I quote first from quoted interview-statements of Professor Stanley Corngold, whose subject is Germanic languages. He presents his students as loosed from ideas of transcendent realities of being (such as Religion attempted to define): "The Other has become the other person, or society." But, it is indicated, mere practicality is an inadequate answer to the problem of knowledge of the self: the new humanism, it seems, has, in getting a grip on practice, lost all hold on 'theory' — itself a new-humanistic deprecatory label for the knowledge of good-and-evil, the understanding of right-and-wrong. The new learning, indeed, has no 'ethos', and because it has begun from nothing, has derided the generality of conceptions of the good and the right, the accumulated inheritance of human testimony to awareness of a principle of good, and of a practice of right implicated with it, as inhering in the very actuality of the being of 'things', of people and things, of Being. Professor Corngold voices the new-humanist spirituality, which is not a conception of values but of a basic valuelessness into which humanity must, with compassion for itself, inject a sensitivity to this valuelessness as an ever-temporary absolute in the terms of which the individual human being can meet with others as 'sharing his predicament'.

Life, says the interviewed professor, is tragic — or a matter for irony: 'one is in time'. The import of this reduction of the human situation to a formula supposedly more satisfying spiritually as a key to a suitable process of self-evaluation in these times than any answer to 'the question "What am I?"' at an empirical level, at the level of the public, everyday self', is that to look for meaning in the situation is folly, but folly committed with dignity. The philosophic substance of the formula consists of the thinnest shavings from a philosophic conventionalism of the literary art of antiquity that has had more prestige in the studiable aggregation of human findings about existence as a pattern of human *theatre* than of human wisdom. The implication, that is, is that the essential consolation for the indignity of human existence, the only chance of personal dignity, lies within the experience of contact with variations on the theme of the tragic nature of life, the irony of hope, the temporal character of time, offered by literary art.

"With the loss of certain illusions, you begin to care for literature." We have, then, here, a substitute for a human learning in terms of direct knowledge and understanding of a comprehensive scope of aspiration that is intended to serve also as compensation for the spiritual inadequacy of empirical knowledge and understanding: the process is a retreat into an imagination-world in which the spiritual patient (immediately, in Professor Corngold's considerations, the Student) enters into a relationship with the text, or, in another phrase of his, "the self that speaks in the text". The scene of this purportedly potential redemptive experience — literature as it is now taught (and, increasingly, written) — is, then, a spacious area of disillusionment made comfortable enough for disillusionment to be enjoyed in leisure as self-enlightenment. All concerned — patients (the student as star-example of one), spiritual diagnosticians (the professor as a star-example), practising therapists (i.e. the literary artist) — are damaged goods, varying kindred examples of the tragedy and the irony of selfhood, teaching or learning or composing the script of the blessed, restorative lesson that they are this.

Now I turn to the new-humanist sentiments expressed by the second interviewed Princeton faculty-member, Professor English Showalter, whose subject is French, and French-European Literature. His academic outlook is not complicated by an assumption that there exists for pedagogy a trustworthy human inheritance of knowledge, a fixed extract of the long human learning to be human, a ground of consciousness of values found unaltering.

I regard universities as a place where society can afford experiments that fail. Failures are educational too. But a lot of universities are opposed because someone isn't sure they will work.

He would like to do away with formal courses, even departments, "just because of the bureaucracy".

A lot of students are interested in problems, like urban studies, race relations, pollution, which are genuinely interdisciplinary. It would be ideal if every student could have an adviser who was interested in the same general questions.

He would like to see, instead of formal courses, lectures or seminars offered whenever the faculty wanted to offer them, for anybody who wanted to attend them. He approves of the university's being committed on political issues. He notes a problem of disagreement between those who have lost confidence in the government, and those who, though they don't like it, don't like to deny it their confidence. The position of this professorial exemplar of 'a new humanism' is a much more loosely-conceived, more informal one than that first considered, and its plane of interest is, as presented, less elevated. But both positions manifest a major common characteristic of new-humanism mentality. It is a mentality that makes *the tentative* its norm.

Whether the interest-focus of a particular new-humanist position is political, or literary, or of art-pertinence, or some other pertinence, it is invariably, and necessarily, of its nature, one that cannot become decided — except in the fluid decisiveness of opposition. It comprises no, begins in no, internal values-commitment of its own. The characteristic contemporary humanism begins and ends at an infancy-point in human intellectual age created by the rejection of the maturity thus far attained in the human course of being. It is a non-critical rejection, rejection of the very idea that there is anything to mature *to* in the human prospect beyond a consciousness of the physiological and physical inextensibilities and extensibilities: all maturity-cultivation, all spiritual values-defining, all 'ethos'-building, is squeezed into this plot of *disavowal* of the aggregated intuition-experience of human beings of a human potential exceeding the suggestions of physicality. The character of intuition itself undergoes change, within the influence-scope of this re-education of human beings out of their intellectually inbred education: it becomes an intuition of the physical — the intuitive process turning back upon itself, swallowing itself. This can be perceived in the educated emphasis put upon sensations-production in contemporary experimental behavior, in the making of nudity a 'cultural' value, in the purposive imbecility of contemporary experimental drama, in which a new dignifying of human existence is presented in the indignifying of it, in which the tragic is at once the comic, in which every theme, be it of life or death, or of good or evil, is reduced to nullity by being cut up into physical chunks and proved thus a meaningless chaos of self-contradictions — in which the dignity of human beings is in viewing themselves whimsically with a theatrical producer's impersonality, as characters all in a play of the no-sense of which they must make their sense.

What of this rebeginning I have written of here, where I am not as in *The Telling* proper speaking out to others as being of an entirety, with me, from which must issue — whatever be the human number of it, the number of the self-chosen — the harmonic voice of entirety, telling its-our story to itself which is ourselves giving it back itself (to be not 'it' but the One of entirety affirmed indivisible in us)? Do I — privately — believe that *any* will rise from the contemporary flatlands to mount the height, with me, of such tremendous and beautiful and real expectation? I composed *The Telling* not so much from a height above as a position of temporal levelness with my contemporaries. I felt, speaking there, *on time*. The others? The most I felt to be hiding from the common immediateness in little evasive immediacies of their own, all pledging community in a vague language of self-concern while defrauding one another of it. I was *sure* of one: my husband Schuyler. He only is specified in *The Telling*: 'one close to me'. I could have spoken so of no other. We knew one immediateness. He knew my immediacy was given to that one immediateness, to which his own immediacy was sworn; and, when there was *The Telling* to read, he found in it omens of the acceptance of his pledge, the welcome of all time to him in his eager generous presence in this far At-Once of human-being which claims us all from ourselves. I can answer for his aliveness to the nature of Life as a course of being continual with courages of rebeginning (we not stopping it in ourselves, with ourselves, for ourselves!). By each's own aliveness to this we perceived it in each other; we were keen-eyed measurers of it in each other, scrupulous against soft indulgence. For no others can I answer. But I need not answer for others in order to remind them who they are, of what make, what our time collects in itself (everything, to be known closely, to come close to!).

In *The Telling* I have shown how the make of being we are destines us to approach one another in an intensifying familiarity of recognition as of *one* make, and that oneness of make no unity of particular race-kind but that there touches in what we are the full of existence's diversity; and how even because of this, and with this, there is upon us a charge of speaking the meaning of *One* that has been as lost in the disguise of silence being has worn, in the dispersion-of-being called the universe. I say this not to return here to the recounting labors of *The Telling*, but only to introduce a declaration of my sense of the reasonableness of thinking that among who are *there will be more* — more of us quickening to consciousness of a practicality of hope eternal in an eternally immediate practicality of rebeginnings. My declaration: Since I consider us, human, to be all of this make, how can I not think that there will be more, though the contemporary hour-on-hour be a self-repeating dead-end, all (is it not all?) running away from further to their individual temporarinesses, none the less if they go in crowds?

A few feel gladness in *The Telling*'s having been written. One, a friend, wishes for just such a supplement as I had originally planned to provide (as I describe in the 'Preface for a Second Reading'); and he pronounces *The Telling* to be what is needed. Another, a friend, prizes it as a thing of its own peculiar kind, without any view of it as something needed. She dislikes all addition to it: let it be there purely, apart in its bare identity, her thought is. I should have stood by my original intention of adding nothing to it had I not seen how *The Telling* became increasingly lost in the solitude of its uninsistence on itself. Further, I found publishers disinclined to print it as a book (after its magazine printing), as being 'too short'. (Many a book of poems makes a slighter volume than it would; yet it confers on readers, in its smallness, place for themselves in it no book of poems could.) And so I have given the little book the company, *in it*, of my private person. This may more move courage in readers for associating themselves with it humanly — its author (as distinguished from this expatiative *I*) seeming less than fully real, humanly, by her idea of a function of human beings, a comprehensive potentiality and responsibility implicit in their human-being, of uniting through themselves, mending in themselves, the cosmically fractured sense of Being.

Who, of those who have read *The Telling* with little more than a bewilderment respectful of its seriousness, wondering, "Dare I believe in her descriptions as well as in the evident utter wholeness of her own belief in them?" will be assisted (indeed, who of those who have not yet read in it at all) in establishing a practical relationship between the book and themselves by this expansion of its occasion with my private presence? Will that make readers feel the work the less remote, but at the same time make it seem the more accommodatable within their world of variant, conflicting, often tantalizingly indistinguishable or similar, often more than graspably different, considerations and interests? — so that what gain there is is one merely of their being the richer in the appurtenances of confusion? I accept the risk, thinking there is, anyway, a time-limit to how long we shall go on failing an appointed knowing by the mind, owning by the soul, speaking by the being, the meaning *One*. Thus says the private person. (But thus also said the author.)

Perhaps what I have written here under this heading ('The Idea of Rebeginnings') will provide so much indication of the intimate thought-accompaniments of *The Telling* that it will chase sympathy, make fear of what they call these days, in blurbish flattery of a mass-cult of seriousness, 'involvement': is this not a costly pursuit? I stress the self, as I have from the beginning of my writing-life done, but I recommend what seems to be a reduction of self. Will not some think: there are, are there not, philosophic and religious orientalisms to which we can lose ourselves with less strenuousness, and only in unfinalities of meditation?

I do indeed mean a final, irrevocable, ridding of the self of all with which it is substanced as a center of social identity. People do not comprehend how much of what they regard as their 'development' — that enlargement of their personal capability of sensitive perception-experience fostered by education made socially available to them — is more a limitation of their selves' essential and ultimate potentialities of being, as human, to their social locale than a liberation of their selves to their reality as forms of being having, beyond consciousness of self as inhabiting a locale, consciousness of self as existing in a universal frame of reference. To know their selves by this unlocalized consciousness of self (possessed by every human being, which goes with being human, and which must be dealt with somehow, because it is there — the disposition of it often a suppression of it, often a mingling of it with the locale-consciousness of self, to its loss of identity in the latter), and to hold to it, and to learn how to clarify and purify it amidst the claims on self of the locale (reclaiming it over and over from the dominance of these): this is self-reduction to the actual measure of personal individuality in an All-inclusive Unity (unity of being), One. The self-reduction I recommend is reduction to being a representative of that One, a speaker of whole truth, truth rescued from the unintegratable, diverse narratives of being sounding within each human locale that makes a world of itself (unspeakable their sum) — and from the pretended oneness of that pluralistic sophistication, that faithless ecumenicity, in which the total sense of earthly residence is rendered as the neutralization of all the variant senses of it.

I recommend a rescue of self from the *littleness* of those worlds which are magnified by their populations of selves from locales into worlds, and cast back a glow of false magnitude upon the self of each of their inhabitants. And a rescue of the self from the largeness of humanity conceived of as an earth-wide Society: this is the lie of fear of one another, by the diverse social locales, dressed flatteringly in mutuality of regard — the single self *loses* human orientation, floating in this sentiment. And rescue of the single self from the vaporous infinitudes of the varied spiritual-intellectual locales that occupy the upper air of the social locales, scattering, gathering, forming, dissolving: the soul, over and over taking that freedom and disorder of cloud-life for its element, is over and over exhausted there of its eternal nature, and falls down to try again, the fault seeming its own. What I recommend for the self is its rescue by its rescuing truth: truth and the self are in the same plight, truth waiting upon self's speaking of it and self wasting its while until it speaks it, unwhole until it speaks it wholly.

But, the more I talk on what I mean, the more I may be discouraging the interest to pursue what I propose. The contemporary imagination beguiles itself with fantasy-tales and fantasy-picturings of human futures. But what I propose will perhaps have the double weirdness of seeming something extremely different from both contemporary and past notions of human destiny, and of treating the postulated different future course of things human as enterable into, or to be entered into, extremely soon. How different what I propose is from that which the self knows and anticipates in its still untainted part — the part untinctured with loyalties to that to which it cannot be loyal — will be a matter only of a private discovery, for those whom I may move to study how different — or like — their consciousness of the given human nature and future, and mine, are. As to speculation on the possibility of entrance into a state of being (whether soon or unpredictably sometime) in which, be it thought of as extremely different or not from the present or any past or imagined

future one, being is rebeginning of being: knowledge as to
this is a matter for mutual verifying, each with the other. For
where Rebeginnings are truly made, the world of indivisible
being — the whole we are, being truly, *the* world — rebegins.
As to this, we are one another's record: we must read one
another.

The idea of Rebeginnings serves as a commonplace of
rhetoric in the history of human changes — changes in
general moral, religious, aesthetic, attitudes, in political
methods, and knowledge-processes. The world is described as
undergoing a rebeginning in this or that manifestation of
change in one or another of the fields of human performance.
We are supposed to have, not very far behind us, in the
explosive consequences of a modernism activated mainly by
disruptive energies, a new genesis of human existence. And
we are supposed to be now poised between the good — albeit
violent — fortune of having lost a reality of being we longed
for but possessed only as a ghost of knowledge of it and the
unassessable fortune of having gained a reality of being firmly
held within the unghostly, at-all-points visible boundaries of
the brief, the just-so-far-and-no-further, the unlovable, life
disembarrassed of the company of the soul . . . Supposed to be
pausing to learn how to be happy in such change. If the
rhetoric of the time is defied, quest of the lovable life can be
renewed in a literal sense of human rebeginnings. In the
account of the idea of Rebeginnings that I have here given,
the journey of varied application and explanation on which I
have taken it, and bring round, now, to its start in literal
reference to my husband Schuyler and myself (who have
vested in it our literal life), perhaps another and another
may find means of stripping that rhetoric from the idea and
letting it have the meaning of their being's love of being. It
would be difficult for me to press possibility beyond that, but
difficult, also, not to press it that far.

MAINLY, EXTRACTS FROM COMMUNICATIONS
(here and there edited)

[As to the spirit — the nature and the working of the spirit, its being 'within' not as if the lodger and we the dwelling-place, but as the whole, which cannot be *outside* . . .
For my husband]

The spirit is not partible into inward instances of its presence. And we can only know the non-partibility of the spirit — how, truly, the spirit is in us — in a sense of its wholeness, though we feel it working within us in its bodily partitude. And so comes the question 'What are *we*?' If we construe ourselves as entities, in our bodily singleness, view ourselves as identical with body, then are we not hindered from apprehending the wholeness of the spirit in us, limited to knowing it as a piece of the spirit? In our knowing the spirit in us we are, ever, straining the body to admit of the knowing (and the body, if we ask our bodies to do their all to forward us as souls, will, indeed, of itself strain itself for this) — and are, ever, losing and gaining apprehension of the wholeness of the spirit in us. We suffer, thus, terrible losses, moment-long, and longer, of this apprehension, the loss terrible and the not-knowing there has been loss, also terrible — for body's confusion is ours, together with its ableness to help us be souls. These are matters of a trembling importance — I hesitate to break them up, speak much of them. For what happens ultimately in this body and soul partnership must be as little as possible interfered with by anxieties of inspection. Our minds mediate between them, in their favoring each other while differing with extremes of difference. The resolving of the contradiction, however, is the soul's work, which it, of its ascendant generosity, alone can do. I press the subject no further, then. Let us — with all our capability of bearing with the distress there is in being human — leave body, mind, soul, to their delicate work of kindness to one another.

As to the 'innocence' and 'curiosity', of which I speak in *The Telling*: there is a danger in their being taken for prescriptions, as if I were saying 'Be innocent, and be curious, and you shall remember what I say can be remembered'. Customary connotations for 'innocence' and 'curiosity' should be avoided: the words belong to no context but that of their own meanings. The innocence I spoke of is the simple innocence of not seeking anything else but the memory. I say 'Pursue the memory' — that is, I posit the existence of a path of memory, in the person, on which to go. For this enterprise the purest curiosity is needed: the object, to discover what is at the end of the path, what is in the memory. Ideas of 'learning about one's existence' do not belong here — they would adulterate the curiosity. I am stressing here the possibility of a recognition in oneself of having a memory (such a one as I mean), and suppressing it. The conditions of discovery are, by my description, very bare, of an utmost simpleness.

As to agreement: we must all transcend the ways of doubt, belief, argument, persuasion. I present what I think are the terms of a unity so broad that nothing good is excluded — I think they are the terms of the good as well. In this I am, I know, vulnerable to judgement as an absolutist — to charges that I provide for too much, in my understandings, that the values of unity are not necessarily the values of the good, and that both can be rules of tyranny. I must transcend my insistentness in representing unity in terms of the good, and the good in terms of unity. You know that I speak so from the mere encouragement of the beat of truth I feel in the words — not of my making, but of the words own falling well, contentedly, among themselves. But I am their speaker, I am, rightly, vulnerable for them. I must transcend my contentedness in their self-contentedness. We must all be ready to say our saying *over*. There is no truth that cannot be better said *over*. Perfection, in truth, and all else, has no single finality: its finality is in infinity. What I say, *you* know, I say with insistence on the words' being at peace with one another. But beyond gladness felt is a gladness I would have in saying the said over, to say it better. May such ease, which is in me, and which love, as we know, nourishes, flower into an assurance in my further words — and in perceptible after-bloom, in what *has* been said by me — that I mean all our ease, in all our words.

[To someone, on 'the step of mind', of which I speak in
The Telling, speaking of the part of women]

The moment will come when the moment, the very moment, is lived as a moment in (or of the life of) the whole-world. The leap of the mind (call it a 'leap' for the difference it will make!) out of the half-world (with its fillings-out that do not fill) to this reality of the whole — which seems merely to impend rather than to be — makes (will make, will have made) Quarrel shed from us all. For in the life of *this* moment (and the next after, and every further one) all are of one life: it is an indivisible moment, it has itself a wholeness of time-nature, so that life in it is not partible . . . Until this moment we are split into life-fragments by our moments — halved and halved and halved into a state of Quarrel continuously renewed under the name of life . . .

[To another, on what there is to do]

To 'write' can be important doing, but always it is incidental to the general human responsibility; it is an intermediation between the coming to know what there is to do and the doing of it . . . There is a force of union with one another to be found, a common meaning of being by which to be. So, what there is to do is, ultimately, a matter of relationship. We have to look for the love of the good in one another, and move towards one another as we see the color of it — and not stop so long as the color holds true. There is a logic governing the work of human relationship. The mutual proving of the love of the good becomes a closer and closer test; and the test is both for error and false hope as well as for rightness in the choice of one another as companions in the perpetuities of the good. That is, in the concern of the one with the other being as I have described, an issue of knowledge in the terms of the human life-principle is assured.

[To another]

. . . how much people divert themselves from the instructions, within, of the human life-principle: the extent of this is how much they spend of themselves in the seeking of safety from self-loss in the sense of a self-abundance that is never measured. The proportion between the wasted and the still unspent is where the decision between self-loss and a sufficient self-saving lies. The life-principle holds this secret, in generosities of extenuation. . . .

[To a friend much older than myself, given to believing
in the reality of 'a lovely side of things']

I see that you made my words welcome — put no barriers between them and yourself. I think the key to an answer to your question about 'remembering' is in your welcoming spirit: I think you do not need much explanation. When you say 'this remembering' you have already faced yourself directly towards the experience as a possibility for you. What is left to do is not 'cultivating' but finding the memory-capacity in yourself as something already possessed. Most protect themselves from their knowing capacities where knowledge seems something burdensomely strange. You make no barriers between yourself and the unknown, no divisions into familiar and strange. For others, 'cultivating' might be of some use. The cultivating would have to be a general spontaneity of response, even to what had been treated as rightly understood in their ideas of things. For many regard themselves as thinking and feeling in free response to what presents itself to them while greeting everything with prearranged responses, unaware how much they exist within the limits of conventionalized attitudes, and how they meet new circumstances or questions of possibility as self-repeating old ones.

You are not afraid of meeting a circumstance, or a possibility, in the simplicity of unguardedness of spirit. Some, capable of such simplicity are diffident in it (there being much in the sophistications of their social environment to make them so), and seek backing for it in what seems its like in the notions of others. Thus, the most uninfected with conventionalized attitudes can be caught up in naive philosophies that conventionalize their natural human simplicity . . .

I believe that you need no assistance with 'this remembering', that you could (and, in ways that have not yet added themselves together, do) produce from within yourself testimony of the spiritual authenticity of your existence (of your going back, in your human immediacy, to Being-Entire). And whoever can do that can suggest to others the potentiality borne in them of doing likewise — a difference of time-understood will be perceived, and spell a past before all pasts to know.

For the present I leave you to your own good care, in these things.

[To another, who had written on horror felt
at evil perceived in a person of close acquaintance,
of whom I had some knowledge]

. . . I believe in no original ultimate evil — evil intrinsic to being. There are mistakes in what constitutes Being, obviously.

I believe in an ultimate self-righting of Being. But there is a before-dawn domain of the human, as dark as night, through which we pass on our way to the human day. And there is in some a wicked will to convert this into a permanent abode. The extent to which a person is absorbed in the effort to materialize the will is a terrific mystery of his own isolate soul (what may be left of it). There is a point beyond which one can't intrude into the area of such a phenomenon — and ought not to try to intrude, because of the danger of harming oneself in the attempt. One must consecrate oneself to the dawn, before it is dawn — and to the Day, in dawn: dedicate oneself to the verification of the possibility of redemption from the less than right, all the degrees of wrong of it, in which Being is less than all-itself. This verification is the most one can do for those who would, for the power of stopping Being short in less than it is, in order to be more than they are, call end what is less than End (as, to call darkness the envelope of day).

[To one whom I saw to be confusing a good
understanding of things with a good understanding
of things a writer should have]

There in every human being a passion for knowledge of the real that is still a stranger, though lying within the scope of one's sense of reality. (In speaking of an unknown, one is describing it as within this scope — present in it, though unknown: were this not so, one would not speak of it at all.) Reality — what is known and unknown, of it — is, must be essentially, for the human being, the human reality. By this I mean, everything within the scope of the sense human beings have of reality, with themselves in it as inherently important to its self-explanatoriness — its self-dependentness. How could it be otherwise, with human beings called upon to be aware of it, and ever calling upon it to make itself all-known? 'The human reality' is, simply, reality as reclaimed by human beings from the non-existence in which it exists for its *things*, and its creatures non-human: by *this* name, it is loved, it is owned — and human beings have lovedness and ownedness in it.

[Now, after I had expressed what I describe above with the phrase 'the human reality', I discovered that the modern existentialist Heidegger had used the phrase to express the idea of 'man' as a being — in the existentialist Sartre's words — which "exists before it can be defined by any conception of it" . . . that "first of all exists, encounters himself, surges up" . . . who to begin with "is nothing" and will be "what he makes of himself." Thus the 'existential' phrase 'the human reality' doesn't mean either reality or human, it means only being called 'human', without presumption of there being anything such as a human nature. *My* phrase means reality real with human awareness of it and its realness, and it means human as pertaining to beings having a human nature, real in its sensitivity to its aware presentness to reality: *my* phrase honors reality and us as of one make and life.]

Reality, then, as the human reality, I consider the natural object of knowledge — human knowledge, knowledge for the pure sake of understanding. Were we purely dedicated in our knowledge-passions, not drawn from that single object to a lesser one or lesser ones for the sake of more quickly come-by praiseworthiness (the desire for approval competing in urgency with the need of understanding), we should seem less skilled in how we knew our reality (the reality in and of which we are), and less proficient in understanding it in knowing it, than are those who labor in the lesser causes of understanding, for the lesser objects of knowledge, that pass for great ones among us. But only because those who choose the lesser causes, the lesser objects, for their great ones, go so fast. And there is no reaching an end in them — no fullness of understanding earnable. But to get to my preachment. For this is introductory to some preachment that your attitude to things literary has prompted me to prepare for you. (And I shall, I think, be wanting to speak in the same sense to others.) I am writing not just to explain my meaning in the phrase 'the human reality'. I want to criticize the making of versions of this reality to fit a specialized interest. Thus, 'writers' conceive of themselves not as human beings concerned (naturally) with the understanding of the human reality, but as writers concerned with having a writer's understanding of the human reality. This amounts to a search for a writer's equivalent of the human reality. There can be no equivalents of it that are not artificial substitutes for it. The same holds for the kind of knowledge that is aimed at in such searching for equivalents: this is as knowledge good only for the creation of substitutes for the human reality.

One comes again and again on the word 'integrity', in connection with writers: integrity is something they are supposed to have, to be good writers. But this is all mistaken refinement of the meaning of 'integrity' and of 'good' — they do not relate, properly, to professional qualities of conscience and sensitivity, as such use has them doing. Conscience and sensitivity, whatever the employment, should be called upon to function by no particular standards, only standards of what is proper to them as *human*. . . . This is the area of your vulnerability, as it is for nearly all writers; but you are especially vulnerable, for you yearn not just for success as a writer but to be of the very best, and such yearning posits a literary reality both equivalent to and superior to (that is, that transcends) the human reality. It is a characteristic of such yearning that the writer feels the success envisaged to be the same as moral perfection, or, alternatively, aesthetic perfection (where literature is viewed as art produced inside the head for enjoyment inside heads) — you incline to the aesthetic side of this professionalized idealism . . . I beseech you to try to cease to look with a writer's eye, think with a writer's mind; look, with your human eye; think, with your human mind; — and, if you write, write as a human being, not as a 'writer'. If what you write is true, it will not be so because of what you are as a writer but because of what you are as a being. There can be no literary equivalent to truth. If, in writing, truth is the quality of what is said, told, this is not a literary achievement: it is a simple human achievement.

Literature being the great mixture it is of all the virtues, vices, capabilities, faults, ambitions, schemes, hopes, appetencies, that words in their necessary union with their users have adhering to them, it is difficult to think of as a field of activity dominated by an artificial version of the human reality: literature seems very 'human' — in the vulgar sense of the word. Further, literature has woven a veil round itself within which the literary reality is reverently shrouded as if it were the real thing; readers and writers commit themselves to the equivalence as to a mystery. That it is a false equivalence few would want to know, for we have all been nursed on the interpositions of literature of itself between ourselves and the reality, and become dependent on them.

If I pointed to how there was something to be called the social reality, a conception of human beings as having their existence entirely contained within its social boundaries, and declared that this was a false equivalent to the human reality, you would not, I think, have much difficulty in focusing on my meaning. It is much easier to see that the social reality is a substitute-creation than to grasp that literary articulateness can be the articulation of a reality that has no reality outside of the special ground on which the articulation has been made ... I am not trying to induce you to abandon your literary pursuits ... Somewhere in its course, literature will come of age as the common ground on which beings speak the — and speak of the — human reality.

Postscript. The growth of dedication to false equivalents of the pure objective of concern with the human reality — concern with it for its entire sake as embracing us, yielding us to

ourselves, and entitled to be served by us with truth in return
— is marked by hugely multiplied involvement in thought-
positions in fields of art, literature, philosophy, assumed as
revolutionarily 'new', besides 'new' political and sociological
stands. The great number of people energetically involved in
the prosecution of newness in diverse fields of interest and
activity suggests a great general enlargement among human
beings of disinterested seriousness about all phases of human
existence, in which the power and prestige of old evaluations
are courageously withstood. The foam of the effect of disinterested seriousness that all this produces obscures, however,
new great underworking forces of *arrivisme*. There is far
more of mere ambition to achieve personal success, the power
and prestige of righteous intelligence, than new stir of dedication to the articulating of the human reality with truth. (The
evidence of the latter is so slight that it is almost impossible to
escape from the accusation, in speaking of it, of making reference to an idealistic abstraction.) Beware of this race going on,
in which the runners wear so many different combinations of
colors, to demonstrate new livelinesses of intelligence. Merely
to be running in the race gives people a sense of success, which
is sharpened by a mutual flattery conferred in the running
alongside one another. This is to be seen on a large scale in the
'cultural exchanges' that go on between nations, these days:
the actual object is not to effect between their peoples a new
understanding of one another as human beings but to attain
in the general world-view to conspicuous distinction in the
display of new potencies of intelligent performance . . . One
hears accents of elevation in the new insistencies. But who are
seen aiming above the height of their own heads? . . .

[To the same, at a later time, on themes
especially dwelt on in *The Telling*]

. . . I see us [human beings] as, nearly, a salvation of the
being or Being out of the rupture (to be seen, plainly, to have

occurred in a Once of it) and reformings of which we emerge
. . . I see how the potentiality of realizing such a salvation in
ourselves is lost over and over again to the sub-uses we make of
ourselves individually. We put ourselves to these uses to
expend rather than fulfil ourselves, the object in this being
satisfactions that must always come, at last, under the sign of
death. But where is the point of departure from the course of
partial fulfilment (ultimately, total unfulfilment) that we have
inherited along with life — departure from the life-towards-
death course? Where the departure *to* the life-towards-life
course — towards life pure? We must find in ourselves the
knowledge, the answer, as truth uttered by us, so distinctly
uttered that we have in it the angle of correction of the misturnings we have made (all the misturnings being correctible
in their sum of misdirection). There is no straight except as we
have no ends-in-life but the fulfilment of the being (the
reality of being, or, the reality, Being) of which we are the
speaking forms.

All our problems as individual beings are in the large the
same as one another's. There is much littleness and difference
to be dissolved, however, before there can be a general
attestation to this sameness — and a general awareness that
all our problems as individual beings have only one same
solution.

[I am moved to refer at this point to a sentiment expressed in
a book of 1937, W. Macneile Dixon's *The Human Situation*,
that corresponds with much in the contemporary mood. ". . .
we are wholly in the dark about everything. Blank ignorance
is our portion. In reasoning from the experience of nature and
ourselves, we have all the evidence there is . . . There
remains, then, the reasoning itself, which is philosophy." It is
the crucial fact of having the experience of ourselves that
belies the naturalness of 'blank ignorance' as 'our portion'.
'Experience of nature' is a humanly irrelevant distinction, a
scientific separation having scientific uses but not a separation

matching our knowledge. For knowledge is our portion, not blank ignorance, in our having the experience of ourselves; and our experience of nature is one with our experience of ourselves.

[Reasoning occurs in knowledge, not in the vacuum of ignorance. And it is the treating ourselves as being involved in a process of knowing, in our having the experience of ourselves, that makes the difference between fullness of participancy in the human reality and defective participancy. The account quoted of reasoning as philosophy mirrors the fallacy (not new, but become widely stylish) that humanness is something of dubious reality, existing less by virtue of itself than by virtue of postulates tentatively sustained in the interest of a sane posture in living the human life.

[And I am moved to comment on the contemporary opposite number to the idea of an intellectual strategy of resorting to the use of reason as the defence against an environment of experience regarded as conducive, by the ignorance it imposes on us (supposedly) in our and its raw, to insanity. This is the cult of a mystical irrationalism — mystical by pretension — that does not worry about ignorance, proffering short-cuts of various kinds to the sense of a reality of mixed make-up, the human ingredient of indistinct identity among the indistinct others in the indistinct whole. This has been called the 'counter-culture'. It is not just a counter-force to reasoning exercises and programmes designed to solve the problem of sanity-keeping, viewed as the main human problem — it is neither afraid of insanity nor in love with sanity. It is 'agin' everything that manifests stability or is favorable to stability (the stability of anything). Whether they like it or not, people have the company of this assault on the 'established' — which is in principle more an assault on the belief in, the certainty of, anything, than on institutions of belief or certainty — dinning in every quarter of their social environment. It dins away in abusive speech and actions, and in journalistic and literary and artistic forms of antagonism, repudiating all concepts of a human responsibility to justify (deserve) humanness in knowledge of what it is. The spirit of this counterdoing, which masquerades as a super-consciousness of the fact of being human, is one of intense, and intensely irresponsible, self-preoccupation, self-fondness. The proponents of it go in grouped formations, but there is the quality of the pack to their unities; each goes for the private sake more than for any common sake. There is a quality of rabble-mentality even in the cogitations of the intellectual hierarchy presiding (haphazardly) over all the counter-doing.

[What is assaulted by the antagonists of the 'established' is criticizable for failure to make the entire environment of human experience the habitual environment: the assaulted complex of constituents forming the daily human world cheats the human reality of much of its due recognition, and so makes human beings live as less than they are. But, in comparison, the life-measure of the human beings, in terms of the 'counter-culture', is of animalistic proportions; the only human reality recognized is the individual reality of each individual human life to its little master-self. This littleness is glorified as the individual unit is glorified in the mob, in there being a multiplied much of it. The extent of the prestige that 'rock' music has acquired as a serious art (the musical performance of the Beatles in modern music held comparable to the work of Manet in modernist painting, by Carl Belz, an art-historian, in *The Story of Rock*; the Beatles found the greatest composers of codas since Beethoven by Alan Rich, a general-music critic — for example) illustrates this glorification profusely. A young German musician, Christophe Eschenbach, has declared that his generation has to love the new music, including 'rock', because "it is all around us, is part of our life". This describes well the spirit of the acceptance by much of contemporary humanity of processes that are vulgarizing — and, even, brutalizing, or, at least, barbarizing — humanness:

seeming inescapable, they are accorded the dignity of being regarded as natural. Many make terms with 'the new music' as a salutary humanization of traditional musicality while not liking it. I suspect that many of these never come to like it, and that more profess enjoyment of it than do enjoy it, and that more are uncomfortable in it than say so.

[The elements of the new music of the young that are regarded as healthily democratic leavening derive from musics reflecting human experience in the humble human circumstance, musics that had an easy force, in which candor, solemnity, and humor mingled, a dignity of their peculiar own. The 'counter-culture' versions of them subvert their emotionality, drown out with their swollen sound the measure of the individual human, small, self-respectingly this against the background of a great universal, to which these musics are attuned. The new sound profanes both the human individual and the universal in its blatant disregard of *proportion*.

[I linger in this aside to point to the glorification of the idea of the individual human being that has gripped the imaginations of such normally public-spirited people as labor for the reform of world-politics. Their imaginations have become stultified in the vanishing from the contemporary field of conceptual thought of concepts in one way or another bespeaking sensitivity to a unifying human reality exceeding in compass the boundaries of those false equivalents to the human reality (indivisible) talked of by me in the presented correspondence-extracts, and outside them. The idea of a 'global village' — the world a cozy assemblage of human individuals — becomes a romantic substitute for political or sociological or other categorical concepts that are themselves substitutes (found inadequate) for a principle of unity, eloquent of a *one* reality, to live by. "Maybe the process of serving the individual rather than the effort of transforming nations will give mankind the universal peace that has eluded us for so long," the Turkish Ambassador to the

United Nations wrote in an article of October 1970 publication (in the *Saturday Review*). Thus is to be observed a conjunction of large-scale spiritual despair and small-scale philosophic optimism, with the good of the particular individual as the emblem of human hope replacing the Good associated with a vision of reality as encompassable within a unified human experience of it as the great single reality of human beings (the human reality!). All the gesturings of conscience enacted on the contemporary stage of concern for the human course have missing from them an inward movement of pride in the fact of the human reality — and a love of knowledge of the Good that sponsors the vision of reality, and engenders the pride. How shame-facedly do the contemporary advocates of a human course ensuring a better human fortune than the present aggregate of individual lots perform their rites of hope!]

[To the same, who raised a question as to a possible likeness
between the views of Nietzsche and my own]

He is so differently disposed from me — so chain-bound to hellish ambitions the imagined realization of which can seem heaven — that (as I see him, and see myself) I assume his sense of reality and mine to be a world — a real world — apart.

[To another]

... To be better at truth-telling is a matter of getting more soul-honor into the use of words.

[To one who wrongly assumed my thinking to have
a like color of opinion to his own because it had intensity,
and so did his opinions]

I saw suddenly, how the very passion to attain to full consciousness and articulate appreciation of this reality (the reality of human existence in the whole) has induced human beings — can induce them, and tends to induce those in whom the passion is most restive — to put what seem to be equivalents of the reality in its place, in their concepts. With the equivalents, which have an easier graspability than the reality itself, they feel that they are giving their passion an objective within reach — the reality itself having an appearance of inaccessibility even at the mind's closest approaches; and they come to identify the equivalent with the reality — the process of equivalence (by which I mean the action of equivalence-making, with all the accompanying effects of it) diffuses the separate sense of the reality, the sense of it as something of intrinsic distinctness. A common example of such an equivalent — which is always necessarily a false equivalent — is the social reality: the actualities of the social existence of human beings are ennobled into equivalence with the entire reality of human existence. Under the spell of this false equivalence a derivative false equivalence is made between the effort to comprehend the social reality and the effort to comprehend the essential reality — the *human* reality.

The field of art teems with 'equivalents' to the reality, and the activity devoted to them is as intense, often, as if it were devoted to the reality itself. (But where there is a false equivalent, the energy devoted to it must eventually become impure at the motivating source.)

There are (people supply themselves with) many substitutes of the reality as a subject of preoccupation, and many compensations for the missing satisfaction of the grasp of it. But I mean to emphasize here neither the mere substitutes nor the mere compensations, but the something into the pursuit of which the ardor of the pursuit of the reality is poured. And, also, I put aside the vulgar (false) equivalents which are mere emotionalisms, and not difficult to identify as such. It is the (false) equivalents that are intellectually adopted and supported that I mean to single out, which might be called the superior false equivalents. These are dangerous deceivers. Yet it might be said that without them the spiritual history of human beings would be a history of poverty. My notion is that human beings have to achieve a certain recognition of their poverty in the spiritual respect, in order to grasp the reality — have to rid themselves of the false riches accumulated in the desire to have something to show and to show to themselves.

. . . I perceived that the processes of equivalence I have described were working in you too. (Please, understand that I consider the processes to be working everywhere.) I shall go on here talking as if talking of fact, but submitting to you a conception, with the idea that, if you see relevance in it to your own thinking, it can be of use to you.

Perhaps you can find the thread of the false equatings that I see by following how your generous movements of alliance with your fellow beings make them as the *denied*, to whom ought to be given the full honor of their humanness. I see such a pattern of attitude as assuming a division of human being into the denied and the deny-ers, and I see those who conform their feelings to such a pattern as dissipating a good deal of their sensitivity to how much there is to be — to have of being — in division between tenderness of fellow-feeling in some directions and hard feeling in others. To go on in this vein: we are all deny-ers to one another of our reality as human beings. To become able to bestow it on one another we must first know that we do not have it in sure enough grasp of knowledge and self-knowledge, yet, to give. We shall have it to give when we have nothing but it.

[To another]

. . . We must think less in terms of personal time than in those of the human life-time. I do not mean that we must futurize, and be prepared to do only so much and no more, posterity taking over where we cease. But, when there's all to do, as I believe there is, of first importance is it, before setting out to try to do, to be sure that all is comprehended within our imagination of all. I think a large part of the work will prove to be the mere learning not to set limits ... The task is not to instal stronger lights, so as to see better in the same places. We must put in an entire new lighting-system, one that covers more ground, illumines places we have treated as not there. That could necessitate our getting along with candlelight or lamplight for a while — and some unambiguous darkness ...

[To the same]

... In this axiom [about people being just people, not kinds of people] one has a formula for one sort of sense of humanness. There is a sense of another sort of humanness, a sense of human beings everywhere (not anywhere, as per the axiom), in the different allocations of existence in which their humanity must struggle to be. The formulation of this sense involves the work-experience of personal cognition of people in their actual diversity-in-the-large — the great humps over which the one-identity human potential has got to climb. The kind of sensibility by which one apprehends such things as the passionate but short-sighted futurism to which the Germans are prone, which shows in their activity and behavior, and the capability the Irish show in their activity and behavior for combining abstractly pure and ecstatically held conceptions of beauty, love, goodness, with light-hearted, conscienceless denials of the truth of the conceptions, is no different from that which, for instance, once can exercise in the perception of the inner condition of [a person known to us both is named].

Suppose one could know every human being in particular and one turned off the process of awareness of them in their large-scale communal diversity. Human beings still, as they now are, one would find, in a total particular acquaintance with the members of a particular large human community, have certain common propensities and peculiarities. Few, few, could be the members of the great English community, for instance, who are so beyond their communal identity as to have attained the state of a non-Englishness of pure human-ness. It is an intricate work, to know one's fellow-beings in the particular, and the large. To my mind, the difference between inflected knowledge of human beings as a com-panion to the sense of human oneness, and generalistic or axiomatic knowledge, is not unlike the difference between patriotism as a loving desire that the people of one's land be their human best and the patriotism of mere pride. In the latter, and in the generalistic knowledge of human beings, there is a lean to over-simplification . . .

Surely, there is nothing wrong with love of country, if that is not your only love. But, as you must know your country to love it, so you must know other countries, to love them. If you are, however, concerned only with persons, not with places, or with people in their large aggroupments, then, travelling the world in mind, or mind and body, you will be continually cutting out the perception of all things except those of where you immediately are. (A where not even of locality, but of private accident only — your where only.) Suspension of the faculties of intelligent recognition of the identity-marks that all people bear of belonging to a particular somewhere on the map of human diversity could clear a writer's — or anybody's — head, for moments, of the prepared seeing and recognizing of people that blots out seeing of them, and knowing what they are. But, generally, whoever or whatever one be, one should take all possible care not to part with one's knowledge — to keep all that one can of it fresh, and at one's side.

I myself do not apply myself to experience as a writer. I do not think of my work as the work of me the writer but as the work of me the worker (a fellow) among all who may be working at elucidations of a certain kind, or, rather, at the problem of all of making mutual elucidations through our truth-potential. 'Writer' is a convenience of social description, and I am not innocent of the use of it. But I have never thought of myself as a writer in the 'artist' sense, which carries with it a tendency to make subjectivity a law ... A footnote as to my work. When I spoke of my work in the Joyce context, I did not have the work-notion of 'my writing' in mind but the notion of my work as work in the field of preparation of spiritually articulate human unity ... When I say 'my', I do not mean to be arrogating to myself special possessive rights in the field. There'll be no success in the field until is is widely and intensively participated in ...

[To another]

Communism is an economic doctrine converted into a general philosophical doctrine. As a philosophical doctrine, however, it never goes far from an economic definition of human values ... There does not exist, to oppose to communism, a different economic doctrine converted into a general philosophical doctrine. One has, in fact, in communism, an intellectual abnormity. Any straight economic doctrine is insufficient for dealing with the pretensions of communism as a general philosophy. The only kind of doctrine capable of dealing with communism with complete ideological justice would be a doctrine of truly universal scope, one in which the diverse values of human good were brought under rational discipline, to the achievement of an intellectual unity of principles effective over the entire range of judgement. No such doctrine yet exists. To assume that it exists in the mere love of freedom and that there is needed but a rousing symbol to convert freedom-lovers into missionaries of a saving universal wisdom is to abandon the intellectual battlefield to the Communists.

[To the same]

... I think no merely political philosophy is going to save the intellectual day, in the contest with Communism ... I think nothing less will serve than a reaching out into the far corners of the domain of consciousness that religion takes for its peculiar own, a completing and correcting of the intellectual substance of the consciousness of a universal reality of principle. The discords of religion have so much splintered the meaning of that reality that it has become more and more lost, there. It is to be found whole where the sensibility that religion has made work for it escapes to its freedom and discovers its own wholeness . . . Communism is an anti-religious and common-sense assault on the grand concepts of the nature of human existence; and religion itself reduces the concept of human nature, and of the human being, to concepts, themselves anti-religious, that argue a given human inferiority, the derogation of the human in them casting darkening shadows on the worshipped fact of the universal genius I call here a reality of principle. — That is, what is needed for the contest with Communism is, also, what is needed for the contest with the Insufficient in spirit with which we minister spiritually to ourselves: we have ourselves, also, to contend with.

[To another]

. . . As to the 'modern' vein, to which I alluded, and those drawings: it was 'abnormity with sexual references', rather than straight sexualness, of which I spoke. I'll condense for you a little essay I wrote on the subject.

A large component of modernism, philosophic, artistic, literary, is the violent, even cynical, break with idealism, followed by nostalgia that plain realism cannot assuage. Fantasy is brought to the rescue — as a method of realism. This combination (intended to endow realism with the mystical appeal idealism has) makes abnormity the measure of the real. Fantasy has no functional scope for anything but the stressing of abnormity, on realistic ground. Where abnormity is presented as true to reality with the help of fantasy, there is no development ahead, no possibility of it — there is only repetition, the monotony of ugliness (the dominant character of abnormity). And so there are added, in the fantastic-realistic vein, from what seems to be creative necessity, sheer inventions, departures even from abnormity, things lacking even the quality of unreality — that have significance thrust mechanically upon them; and all this addendum — accidentalism, one might call it — has the function of serving as substitutes for the beauty impossible to the work. Such procedure (a widely and variously followed one) plays tricks on the intelligence . . . and on human hope. Where it is in force, there is nothing truly good to show, truly true to say. The very fantasy involved is a cruelty practised on human aspiration. Those who use such procedure vary greatly in talent. (Joyce I hold of their number.) Talent, for me, does not justify it. Indeed, by talent the procedure can be made to perpetrate extremes of abberration from the path of hopeful instincts. — I think those drawings belong to the category of such procedure. Also, that other piece: it, curiously, to my sensibilities, tries to be something else, as it goes, but hasn't force enough to do more than stop short as what it set out to be . . .

Now, I see more than frequently, in those who devote themselves to expressive activities, a very strong admixture of ambition of power (power of a character peculiar to the field of these activities — to fascinate attention) with pure expressive motivation. It has got out of hand, it is not merely attendant: the two have become so much mingled as to be hardly separately unidentifiable . . . the former so much in the ascendant, and so much equated with the latter, that sensitivity to its nature, its greedy presence, is dulled. It would be mistaken to think it present in smaller degree in any particular milieu — the non-commercialistic milieu is as heavy with it as any commercialistic one. Everywhere in the literary and artistic worlds it is indulged as a human common-place — there is no emotional or intellectual provision for its not being there. It pulses, in unchecked excess, in all the successive 'new' writing, differing from the more conventional professional aims of arousing interest, exciting admiration, in its anarchic abandon. The numbers of power-aspirants democratically multiply, the degree of demandingness rises, rises. Where a vice ceases to be covertly pursued, the consequence is not innocence: there is more of it. I think the worlds of literature and the arts, of the present, have been considerably indoctrinating the inhabitants of the world-at-large in the vices of indiscriminate pursuit of potency of self . . .

[To the same]

. . . I believe that there is for each and all a new story to tell, a story of which the old — what we keep telling one another in the incertitude of varying repetitions — is not more than some chapters of conjecture prolonged into a book, and a book, a usurping of all our occasions of truth . . . Some, I think, will leave it at that, at the old, not really begun, story, to go on with which seems a feasibility while to tell the new story, the one that begins true, seems impossible . . .

[To the same]

. . . This proposing a choice of belief between a doctrine of free will and a fatalistic doctrine of automatic existence, in which one's course is made for one, I view as the concealing of an actual problem from oneself in a fictitious one. The question is, not how to think, about one's actions, how they are controlled, by oneself or by forces acting on and for one, but what to do of what one sees to do, which of the possible actions are in the field of right, which in that of wrong. The fatalistic attitude is seated in an unwillingness to determine one's actions. The choice of a belief in a fatalistic doctrine is a freeing of oneself (an attempt at this) of a resented responsibility for determining them (the resentment, one of fright, I think — so that the attitude 'What will be, will be' is greatly false bravery, an empty stoicism) . . .

The problem as to one's actions, of what to do in this case, in that, is the incidental manifestation of one continuous problem: what to be. Each particular case is but a form of the whole in a state of continuing unresolvedness. If one makes the choice implicit in an acceptance of one's humanness, then one's problem is, generally-particularly, without distinction of instance, how to attain to perfect being, to have life perfectly ... Then, whatever one does, it is this effort that counts (counts *in* one). This effort will always predominate over one's actions as the actual character of one's life ... Any other kind of understanding that one may make with oneself as to the conduct of one's life can only be, as I see us in our being human, animalish: one locks oneself away in the physical individual fact of oneself as a means of escaping the pains of human choice. Yet for a human being that position is, in every moment of the occupancy of it, all-painful, without escape in *it* from pain ...

You speak of the settling of crucial questions as 'ages ahead'. In speaking so you disregard the speedy deterioration that is going on in the development of the human self, I consider. The current activities of self-investigation, of the pursuit of self-consciousness for self-consciousness's sake, I judge to be animalish in their orientation, and the good objective ascribed to them by those who sponsor them and those who adopt them to be a superficial, pseudo-human imitation of ideas of good rejected as out-of-date, inadequate. The losses in human consciousness of a knowable Good are mounting fast now, I think, above past gains: we are in a total human crisis, in which are all 'the ages ahead'.

[To the same]

I want at least to keep open, in words, the subject of holding oneself undismayed, which you lifted into position between us — and, oh, how glad I am that you did. — There is an area, a ground, a point, a life-place, discoverable within the precinct of the being of some which is both very purely of the person, and also *not* the person as he or she circulates in areas where circumstance changes him or her in varying ways and degrees into its creature. This area is discoverable not by searching but using a knowledge one has, a knowing what it is to be 'there', knowing where it is. When one is there, one is, in being oneself, not oneself alone. One is not of this or that personality-coloring, is not a lone peculiarity among others. One is not that 'poor' this or that one, varyingly unsuccessful and fortunate among others: one is one's being. There's a second-hand car-dealer who speaks ingratiatingly on the radio, maddeningly so to me, saying, of his 'wonderful' service, "It's that simple!" — So, I can't say *that*. But there is, in what I am talking of, simplification of an advanced order, simplification at the other end from the simplicity of not knowing what to do (about trouble) and leaving the solution for providence, or despair (the latter as having a limit, and so a built-in safety).

What I am talking about is a 'there' where the person can always find himself or herself — and be found. A place that, though one is there one's own being, is not a private sanctuary but *the* place of being, *the* where of which the person has come to know . . . In that place, where one is one's being, one is the place, is of the place: we realize here in ourselves the one-spirited nature of being. And are in this (couldn't be other than) not alone . . . though, by the measure of experiment of another sort, one might seem uncompanioned. — Finally, for just now: the body takes the wear harder than the mind: this reflection may be useful.

[To another]

As to passage *9*. Perhaps if I were to write on the subject of that passage now I should try to trace the course of 'mere' evasion, art or strategy, to what now predominates: the evasion has now graduated into its mature life of active discarding (the ultimate responsibilities, etc.). I have been trying to get something written on the drear Women's 'Liberation' activity of the present social moment; and I used, in describing the intellectual pseudo-revolutionary trend, the figure 'going to the Concept Dump' — the women joining the men in junking past concepts (in which are some inklings of the Realities) in the name of intellectual (and etc.) freedom. — Yes, there are some who are neither-nor's. They reflect the fact that there are no leads being given from the usual quarters of authority that take anywhere.

. . . I see Capitalism as *not* a planned, devised system in the sense in which Communism is that. I see it as a complex of inter-related experimentally developed procedures, much confusion embraced in it, with some order (variously) imposed for sheer continuity's sake. I'd like to take this further, some time.

As to passages *18, 19,* and 'Good'. I consider this myself at least a raising of the words out of the mire of culpable human ignorance. At least the mire can start dripping off! . . . Without a placing of spirit, 'spiritual' would be unredeemable, of course. My working 'spirit' up out of the mire has enabled me to use the adjective without hesitation, in my expression, generally.

As to *26*. There is much danger of misunderstanding me in identifying my 'position' of *The Telling* with the position of another or others, an implied identity being read into what they have not explicitly written. The writer who has escaped from spiritual formalism into a broad pagan freedom of fatalism, where hope and despair can be experimentally countered to each other or combined, is neither closer to nor further from my 'position' than those who think in terms of existing types of spiritual formalism. The special sense of what I *say* is lost if it is read into the *unsaid* of others. The danger I see as twofold: myself and the other are both misunderstood, are got askew in the drawing of a straight line of relevance between our thinking, and you in your intermediating thinking can lose the advantage of full perception of the difference.

To dwell a moment on the position of the free-ranging fatalist who has, in dissociating himself from various types of position, taken stand as in an impersonal negative, a grand impartiality, as if the existence of such a position were cosmically plausible and reasonably, to the advantage of wisdom, and furtherance in truth, assumable. This is a private experiment in spiritual ratiocination given literary form, it is not a speaking to fellow-beings from a position of experience in the common urgent life of spiritual experience. I have the view that such evaluations as *The Telling* brings into expression can be useful in comparative thinking only in respect to general types of human activity in the field of spiritual enunciation. That particular fatalism is critically relatable to a general type. But I think the sense and significance of those (my) evaluations will be diffused, if not lost, in indirect application, specialistic comparison, for it is their peculiarity to be *general* evaluations. In this is their worth — what they have of worth. Comparison of them with other general evaluations might be useful; but as values for particular critical application they can only have a partial — and a somewhat forced — relevance, with their general applicability constrained within the context of the particular.

. . . Just a little as to the possibility of deriving from *The Telling* a formula for practical procedure, as for example, a resolution as to proceeding in one's day, days, with close regard for others. There can be an emphasis on 'others' that drains reality from the necessary realness to us of the One that ever walks along with us in our path (in alternate guises of memory and anticipation) — a de-intensifying of the sense of the Extraordinary Situation we are all in that *The Telling* is meant to enliven . . . Resting on others-consciousness (consciousness of others) could make the achievement of Soul-memory the harder! — even in one's new moments of recognizing it as something for one's achievement . . . 'Others' are not quantitatively the same as, do not make with us a sum of, the One. *One* must be known to us before others can have practical realness to us as figures of oneness . . .

[To the same]

As to 'everlasting life': I make no, mean to make no, as-it-were brand-term of belief in my use of the phrase. I am aware of its religious associations. But that does not destroy its functionality as expressive of straight meaning — nor (and this is an aside) are those who make a stock-use of the phrase necessarily 'wrong' in everything the phrase is used by them to denote. I see the human self-consciousness as everywhere impregnated with (what I take to be) a *knowledge* of a force of permanence in (animate in) human being. How speak of this? At that point in *The Telling* the loose identification 'instinct of everlasting life' was my way of being 'honest' with, and kind to, those who might read: anything less loose might amount to a 'putting over' of something 'on' them — I must not give them a 'package' of a detailed ideology of immortality. This is delicate ground, the most delicate, on which each must make the (even, at first, painful) first footsteps before we know one another there. I do not mean to stop questioning, with these words. I believe, I say to you, in this particular questioning-instance, that the labor of *lasting* becomes indeed of a substantiality putting identifications in terms of 'body' or 'matter' into an exterior shade. Let me for the present desist here . . . It is not easy speaking. And I do not present myself as more than a novice in such (not unpainful to me) foot-stepping. As to 'grace'. I quote no theological term. I mean that which one naturally has for possessing in beautiful unity of person the selfhood that makes 'being human'.

As to the soul-memory. This for me (and I mean not in the sense of idea, or belief, but historically, as from my beginning I have lived experiencingly) is my first knowing. I think it is in all of us, but crusted over with consciousness of the later. No, I do not mean it as a metaphor. Use your spatial immediatizing of the conception of our being more than body, matter, to 'place' our temporality in its setting of an initial Being-state, which could not be sucked into, or cast off by, our temporality, but necessarily, in so far as we 'are', comes along with that, is 'there' around that as the very cosmos of temporality. Here again I am going to beg off, with but a short comment . . . The experience is hard to come by as recognized experience, even where the sense of 'Before' is, as it has been with me, one of the gifts of the Cradle (but I must immediately say that I think it is in every Cradle — but is overlooked, is crowded out by Toys).

As to 'Who are *we*?' I face this question of Number at the end, do I not? I have faced it throughout my laboring. There was an English painter called Christopher Wood who made pictures of a pressing vividness. He threw himself before a Tube train. And, as I remember (I can hardly have it wrong, having carried the memory straight along), the note found on him read "Do they know who they are?" — There is no 'I' here, and no 'we'! The 'they' is tragic . . . There is no proof in mere 'I'. In discovering who 'we' are, who constitute a true 'we', adequate to the reality-content of Being, is the only 'I'-proof . . .

As to this current so-much-used, and used as if in the use were established new meaning-sensitivity, 'identify with': it is one of the destroyers, in the air of speech, I think, of faithful thinking. I mean nothing that this self-emptying intransitive could express — no 'identifying with' others. In identifying ourselves each self as of the One that all-is, we utter 'I' in the midst of a 'we' with the whom of which we can all together identify ourselves. There is a certain watchful provisionality called for as to 'I' and 'we', a mutuality of testing: shall I say, a very great necessity of love? — Let it be here tentatively said, tentatively, because I mean to posit no conditions for an ultimate good issue of this humanness.

136

[The following piece of writing is a postscript-commentary on the question of the Devil raised in a correspondence conducted between a young poet and myself in the thirties: there was mention of the Devil in some of my poems, and my correspondent inquired as to my meanings. My letters of this correspondence were, with disregard of me, sold; but, there being regard for me at the point of their acquisition, it has been possible for me to add to the available record they constitute observations of long afterwards on pertinent subjects and circumstances. What I thus wrote on the subject of the Devil bears on things treated of in *The Telling*.]

I have carried with me, from earlier years, the problem of the identification of the Devil. My poetic treatment of the problem was part-personal and part-religious — religious in the sense of my attributing to the Devil the character of a general force. I did not, in that treatment, resolve this ambiguity. I tended to literalism in so far as I made personal identification of the devil-force (seeing it as personally embodied). My difficulty was centered in the question of the nature of *human* identity. For a long time I was discontented with the identification 'human' as applied to beings my hope of whom, my sense of whom as having a destiny lodged in their being, went to the farthest. Attempting to resolve the confusions of meaning that the word 'human' has, in usage, bundled up in it, I made it definitively restrictive in meaning: that was 'human' which fell on the near side of a dividing-line between the historically variable life of people, in which changes were ever rung on the physical and external actualities of the human state, and the final perfect state of being, sparks of the reality of which tingle in the consciousnesses mainly preoccupied with the things of the life on the near side of the line. Neither the concept of divinity nor any other naming-concept (such as that of superhumanness, for instance) fitted, for me, the character of the state of being, and *its* actualities, on the far side of the line.

Ultimately, I had to break with 'human' as meaning everything coming within limits set by the falling-short, of human beings, of the very qualities of identity distinguishing them as a kind, and a not merely animal kind. And in so doing I not only gave myself a word: I rescued the word from its depravity as one in which numbers of incompatible meanings were conglomerated (a depravity having a correspondence with the existing human life-condition as one comprising a variety of departments many of which are incompatible with one another, the components of *these* being themselves much at odds with one another).

Before going on with the subject of the Devil, I pause over the word 'natural' and the concept of nature on which it rests. This word also has suffered of being a vehicle of incompatible meanings, to a larger extent, even, than has 'human', but perhaps with effects less damaging to the view human beings take of themselves, since thinking is on the whole more vague on what is natural than it is on what is human. At any rate, both words have been made the instruments of a conception of human beings of themselves as existing within a range of typical possibilities that, whether defined in terms of natural happening or of human happening, categorically, restrict the very vision of what is humanly possible — and naturally possible — to less than a whole hope, hope of a whole virtue, of partaking of the whole reality of being. In breaking, as I have described, with the meaning of 'human' as a compound of varying meanings held together by human inconsistency and instability themselves (this meaning being the picture of how, mainly, people live), I broke at once with the similarly conditioned meaning of 'natural'.

A sentence in one of my letters of the correspondence the conversion of which into an open document has prompted these later comments illustrates the status of both 'natural' and 'human' at that time in my spiritual lexicon. "Yes, 'Short Of Strange' is very difficult. It is 'about' the falsity of 'progress' within the natural cycle and the insanity of [the view of the] human limit as [the] extreme [reach of existence] with which [living in the terms of] this cycle is permeated." It can be seen how 'natural' and 'human' are associated as specifying ranges of existence that do not take in enough. There is (by this meaning-treatment of the words) no true ascent in the grades of nature — nothing becomes a fully representative articulator of the essential actuality, being. And the human degree of elevation of being, the extreme that is the conceived highest mark of human attainment, is of the same false height as the various high marks on the being-scale of the natural world. — How I was then using these words was one way of using them with consistency of meaning. There was only one other way of using them with consistency of meaning — and to that way I eventually came. But so to use them, both of them in senses which are governed by a necessity of utterly good far implications — this requires a spiritual literalness in all one's conceptual thinking that leaves no loophole for suspended precision.

Now to speak of my present view of Devilishness, which reflects my discovery of the potentialities of 'human' as a word of exclusively good spiritual implications, and literally far-going meaning. In the course of my thought over the years, the matter of the Devil, and the matter of good and evil, with which it makes one piece, emerged from the penumbra of mingled intuitions into the light of deliberate consciousness of these things (which it is impossible not to see somewhat, their reality being ineludible). Evil I had never found satisfactorily placeable as an integral element of the universal, or total, content of existence. Indeed, evil is evil just because there is no logical place for it, no room in reality for it. It is unreal, and yet real as something unreal. I have always, since I began thinking about evil, its being a force, yet a force empty of reality, made of nothing, capable of effecting only nothingness, having nothingness as its province, and yet being 'there', placed it — placed its queer manifestation of itself as something — near or in and around the 'human': that was where I expected to meet with it — if I was to meet with it directly. There was no Manichaean dualism in my conception of the matter of good and evil; I believed in the past, as I believe in the present, that in a remotest heretofore a comprehensive event of the order of division occurred, but that the generative circumstances behind what now is were not the consequence of the operation of a principle of good and evil, light and darkness.

I wrote in 1930, in a little piece published in a book of mine of miscellaneous pieces (*Though Gently*), thus, on The Problem of Good and Evil:

> The problem of good and evil is not the problem of good and evil, but only the problem of evil. In opposition to good there are evil characters, but there are no good characters in opposition to evil. Evil is arguable, but good is not. Therefore the Devil always wins the argument. And the inarguability of good is demonstrated in the plausibility of evil. But what is to become of the Devil, or, to speak accumulatively, the evil characters, after all the arguments are won? He must get out of the spotlight of interest, and yet he has nowhere to go. He must disappear from himself. He must become commonplace. Perhaps he devotes himself to an expletive sophistry on behalf of good . . .

This was written not long after I had encountered someone whose personal character and behavior evoked the identification 'the Devil': I was satisfied that I had seen devilishness. Since then I have seen it again, both in retrospect, where I had missed seeing it, and in immediate recognition; in the latter case, the appearance has usually been in forms not remarkable, dramatically, forms easier to associate with facets of the person's behavior than with the person's character in the round — but always the manifestation has been at least temporarily so vivid that the identity 'Devil' has suggested itself like spontaneous truth. I think it a probability that were one to make a concentrated effort to discover personal examples of devilishness, one would find the number devilishly large: one would meet the Devil — over and over — here, there, everywhere.

Concrete perception of the intervention of the Devil in human life, as a prober of its susceptibility to the influence of Evil, is an eventual necessity: ultimately, human beings must capture the reality of their being subject to spiritual undoing within the immediacies of ordinary, verifiable experience. Devil-recognition goes beyond the homely sense of having done wrong in a wildly pertinacious manner that people express in the proverbial "The Devil got into me." And it goes beyond the grand devil-portraiture of literature, which draws its lurid plausibility from the imagination of the supernatural.

Although I did not often touch directly on the matter of evil, in my poems, and did touch continually on the matter of good, directly and indirectly, and in continually varying ways, in my poems and elsewhere, there was correspondence between the kind of expectation I expressed, in regard to both. I was committed to the expectation that good would resolve itself in human experience — or, rather, that it would be resolved by human life — into self-evident and self-aware forms of personality: I had the prophetical conviction that good was destined to assume the reality of being *persons*. And I had a like conception of the fate, in human life, of evil, which always, for all people, had hovered in fearsome forms close to the borders of the known: evil would 'out', would be visible as persons, be personally knowable. — But whence came evil, which exists only to say nay, and so must pass? Of good, one does not ask whence it came, only why it is not there when it is not. After I had left the gross word 'human', and taken stand upon the word 'human' that distinguishes the qualities of being that make the kind emblematic to itself of good, I knew where to look for the origin of evil.

'Outrageous blarneyman', I called the Devil in a poem:
the name is indeed for a creature of the human world. In the
little prose piece I have quoted, I speak of the Devil reducing
to a poor human figure. There is nowhere for the placing of
the Devil, there is nowhere for the location of the origin of
evil, except the human world, except the area of human life.
This is not clearly thinkable until one has faced the implications of the contradiction existing between the two different
quarters of meaning to which the word 'human' keeps —
rather, is kept — alternately turning. There is a bad quarter of
meaning, and a good quarter of meaning; and, while the good
quarter of meaning is the seat of the unifying sense that makes
the word a term of the highest descriptive importance, the bad
quarter of meaning is the seat of the senses that contest the
validity of the word in its good-quarter character as a practical
description, and contest it with ample evidence of human
failure to meet the ideal of good. But the ideal is human; and
even the failure is human if effort has been strained to meet
the ideal. The bad quarter of human action, which feeds the
senses of the bad quarter of the meaning of the word 'human',
is not a human quarter at all, by the good-quarter meaning of
the word 'human'. It is a usurpation of some of the area of
human life, which is the area of potential attainment in
individual being of entire goodness of being, for perverse uses
of it. And the devilish make of it a sanctuary for identity-less
being. Nowhere else, in the cosmic multiplicity of kinds of
being, besides where humankind is, can something be and be
as nothing, free of the reality of belonging to the kind to which
it belongs. And, everywhere else, the determinations of the
limits of kind have been completed. In the human fold of
being, the distinction of kind is to transcend the kinds, and the
state of being provided for the kind is an open state, not a
closed state. Here, the fulfilment of the nature of the kind
must be voluntary; the identity of kind is not imposed by
necessity, but is the choice of virtue. And here, and here

alone, evil resides, in the persons of all who pretend to possess human identity without having chosen it or tried to choose it. And the Devil is the personality of this inhuman humanness.

[I carry the argument as to good and evil, humanness, devilishness, a little further, a little later.]

Human behavior and character cannot be all subsumed in the dichotomies 'good and evil', 'good and bad'. There are to be distinguished two categories of negative identification — which, however, do not exist in a dichotomous relation to each other; both are characterized by dissociation from the 'good and evil' principle of moral identity. To the one belong those who are dubious of 'good' as the form of success of the human because so much folly and hypocrisy have been committed in the name of it. These are as strivers after good by another name. They seem dedicated to the impossible, relatively to the familiar identifications of 'good', even to an immoral — because pursued by them as outside the norm of human moral aspiration — perfect. In their negative extraordinariness there is, however, so much fierce resistance to possibly corruptive alliance with the suspectable (whatever name it has) that among them are to be found human beings of exceptional purity of human identity. This purity is not of the nature of the Nietzschian superhuman 'beyond good-and-evil'. *That* is super-diabolic, the truly impossible. This is, by the sacrifice of moral self-identification, of an open moral name and credit, a painful and beautiful secrecy. The secrecy, however, reveals its implicit commitment to the perfect, as the only good matching the human sense of 'good', by the furthest sense of 'human' from the ambiguous. *These*, that is, become recognizable, through the brilliant intensity of their unnamed dedicatedness, to lovers of good, as lovers of it in stern refusal to love what may be less: these are themselves to be especially loved.

Now to speak of those of the second of the two categories of negative identification that I have brought into my review of my thinking on devilishness and humanness. These are characterized, as are those of the first category, by dissociation from the 'good and evil' principle of moral identity. They are jealous of their human identity without moral feeling in the jealousy. They cling to it almost desperately as a position of precious advantage; they do not forswear good, but they make no endeavor to know or practise it except as the necessities of self-preservation exact. They do not prosecute a principle of human enmity, no more than they do a principle of human loyalty. They take friends as they can make themselves among them their first or great friend; and, beyond the effective area of such sociality, they will break any humane law for self-advantage, if the risk is much smaller than the chance of that. Such is the personality of the wicked, as distinguished from the devilish. They make a very strong impression of humanness — that mingledly attracts and repels — by the intensity of their lusting after the temporal perquisites of humanness. One cannot think of these as being reduced to the commonplace, becoming what are called 'nobodies'. They are too grotesquely substantial in their hoarded human identity to undergo other reduction than that of a magnified mortal collapse.

Those whom I have described as 'the wicked', who are radically distinct from 'the devilish', tend to be publicly conspicuous, either as figures of fame or of notoriety, while the devilish tend to play their rôle in the private haunts of human life.

(If I seem to have been speaking as from a viewing-platform at the edge of the human scene, and not from a personal stance within it, this is not from any distantness of experience, of that of which I speak. The human scene *moves*. In my thinking, my speaking, I have been moving with it — all move with it, but not all move with it in their thinking, their speaking — and, also, looking back on its historic personality-forms, which recur. I am distant from my subjects only in that they are humanly very old ones, and, it has seemed to me, well-known ones as both old and of immediate content, and needing thus no personal exemplification by me.)

[Finally, I present again, as I did in the preceding, some quasi-epistolary matter. It is a statement I prepared for tape-recording by a business visitor, to be in lieu of something of the order of a writer's disquisition on contemporary subjects in the field of literature, philosophy, and so on, he wished from me, which I declined to provide. Relenting somewhat, I wrote the statement for my speaking into his tape-recorder as a little personal gift. The speaking did not come to pass, for his machine broke down. I gave him for a gift the script itself. Later, at my request, he sent me a copy of it. (*He had, during a passage of silence, asked me suddenly, and surprisingly to me, whether I was happy. While it seemed to me a question of perfunctory and random choice, I answered it with my swiftest in serious simplicity of truthfulness, to keep the occasion clear of conversational dallying irreverent to the subject of happiness. I said: "I am happy in my continuing relationship with my husband." To this the visitor made no reply-comment. My sense of there being between him and myself, instead of a common subject 'happiness', a separating blank, induced me to attempt to address him on the subject to an effect perhaps of more use or interest to him than my brief factual response to his question could be—and of some use or interest to those whom he or chance might make audience to the envisaged recording.*)]

You have asked me about 'happiness'. Happiness is necessarily related to a consciousness of something *good* of which one is sure. The degree of happiness is according to what this good comprises. If it comprises what relates to a personal condition of oneself, it is a limited happiness, subject to modification or even reversal — in the longest run, necessarily so. If it is a happiness centered in a non-over-ridable essential (not over-ridable by any particular fate of a particular happiness), it is one's happiness forever. The good to which it has reference is one's norm of being! One has discovered wherefrom one stems and whereto one finally relates. Notions of happiness have surged in and around human life, flooding the empty spaces in it vaguely, or, gathering substance, sometimes forming islands occupiable for mortal whiles . . . or they (notions of happiness) are erected into subjects of contemplation, instead of being set in the actual human scene. It seems to me that present preoccupation with happiness is broken into molecular notions of individual happiness, or into blocks of such notions, that lack both a romantic, subjective duration, and, even, a practical mortality (mortal existence). My concern is with our consciousness of the essential good, and our sureness of ourselves in our sureness of it. What to call it? I try to 'call' it in *The Telling* in the simplest terms. Other descriptions of it can be found, as consciousness of it grows more determinate.

4

SOME NOTES, ENLARGING ON SOME FEATURES OF THE TEXT

[I limit myself to 'some' notes, having more in reserve, so that there will be no effect made, in this last section of supplementary matter, of my speaking here in conclusion. What I have chosen to 'leave over' I regard as belonging to a continuity of preoccupation with the concerns of *The Telling* as themselves belonging to a continuity in which all who will have travelled with me to *The Telling*'s close, and then lingered with it, and with me, will be with me embraced. Thus, I shall have fulfilled two proprieties that *The Telling* has seemed, contradictorily, to call for: shall have cut myself short in what can be said within the precinct of its name, for immediacy's sake, and have gone further in it, for further's sake — to give assurance to those wanting not to stop that I too am moved by sense of the need and room for more.]

1 · passage 7
"... their wisest words ... do not live ..." That is, they are experiments in saying, things said for the time-being. Whatever lives is informed with the intention to endure, in it is secreted the expectation of enduring. But the philosophic statement is characteristically truth tentative; it proposes itself, but does not give itself.

2 · passage 8
"... a scientist, pining for some old-fashioned philosophic generalization ... will make himself a brew of it, become

himself a philosopher." Jeans, and Eddington, rise up readily for citing. But Whitehead? — 'Old-fashioned philosophic generalization' — *he*? His is only a more aggressive philosophic sentimentalism: for the live nature, the organic unity that he opposes to the inanimate, automatically busy universe of science, Whitehead makes himself spokesman, interpreter, provider to it of self-understanding — a founding member of the universe's university.

3 · passage 9

". . . our treacherous time . . ." Time here is time as consisting of the human substance of all the living taken together. (That is, all who can in their individual substance be taken together as Human Life make 'a time'.) And the spirit of a time is conceived of here as the collective manifestation of Spirit in the total human substance of the time: this manifestation itself invites the word 'spirit', for, manifesting Spirit's working, it itself moves. In many of the uses of the word 'spirit', the working of Spirit is thus identified with its effect — even to the characterizing as 'spirit' persistencies of evil sort, though Spirit itself, the all-affecting Persistency, is in its whole working absolutely and finally good. (For instance, the phrase 'the spirit of revenge' has equal linguistic validity with 'the spirit of forgiveness', while the general notion of spirit — as capitalized in 'Spirit' or adjectivalized in 'spiritual' — is inclusive of connotations purely good only.) I call the spirit of our time self-contradictory because Spirit works perceptibly in the human substance of it to effects diametrically different, and self-confounding. All the potential of good and evil pent in the living substance seems to be activated: human beings are summing human beings, all the human possibilities — what the human ages have variously shown of what can be — are thrown together, and the result is both everything and nothing. From these people-of-our-time we are, we may hope everything, yet have nothing! The time is an end-of-world time, an end of time. We are moving in it, it is not moving. Or, if there is movement, it is a racing in the track of former movement; its forwardness is an infinity of repetition; our progress is an ingrowing into ourselves; our 'new' is engulfed in history as we launch it — no future issues from our time to invite, and receive, the new; our future is a distillation of old futures, and the new we present to it is an improvisation on all the once-new that drifts still life-like in history. *But, if, truly, we move,* our movement is a going-on that parts us from the world of history, in which we live in self-destructive difference from ourselves, and takes us into the world of truth. *There,* we are what we are congruously, humanly; and our self-sameness in time will make the succession of times less and less a rhythm of death. — I have gone beyond the limits of passage *9.* This note should be read again, separately, as a note to the whole of *The Telling.*

4 · passage 11

"Truth rings no bells." That which 'rings a bell', as the saying goes, excites, according to the implication of the saying, admiring wonder, brings one fast to wrapt attention. But, while the tendency is to treat the proverbial bell-ringing thing or being as something exceptional, one knows nothing except that one has been forced to give ear — or eyes or mind — to an insistence. An advent of truth will not provoke wonder, admiration, forcefully seize attention. Truth's nature is to fill a place that belongs to it when the place becomes cleared of a usurping occupant. It slips into place, then, with a quiet of natural fitness, perfectly not-astounding in the rightness of its being there.

5 · passage 11

". . . we shall have the force of truth in us . . ." I mean, by 'that of us which sustained us in false notions of our truth', the will to have our truth, which, acting in separation from our discretion of truth, gave us over to the first belief met, or the next or the next, so that the closest we came to truth was doubt. And I mean, by 'that which sustained us in our waiting for our truth itself', this discretion of truth that the will to truth has from the beginning of our truth-expectancy ever deserted — but that never yet has deserted us. Our discretion of truth keeps us alive through belief and doubt; what we have to say to one another, in truth, is secreted in it from our own neglect of it as we run with our will to truth after the plausible. When our will to say is freed from our wilfulness, and comes seeking what is in us to say, then we shall have the force of truth in us. Such is my sense, here.

6 · *passage 16*

The characterizations Occidental and Oriental are in underlying reference to the mid-nineteenth-century 'Western' origins of Communism and the early-twentieth-century Russian stamp put upon it, as an Oriental stamp. In each case, there was a reversal of a dominant philosophic trend, by a force acting from within its general temperament-frame. The resultant combination, of abruptly modernized Westernism and abruptly modernized Orientalism, is incapable of self-consistency; it is mainly ill-spiritedness that holds the elements of the combination together.

7 · *passage 17*

I say 'of a procrustean male sort', here, because I conceive the motivation of this 'humanitarianism' to be repressive, and to arise in the male quarter of emotionality; its Good is a pattern of antagonism to which everything must be fitted — and antagonism I regard as a prime element of maleness. The all-male quality of Communism and of 'reactionary' totalitarianism is so obtrusively evident that it overshadows the differences in their versions of humanitarianism.

8 · passage 20

Martin Buber, the religious dialectician, speaks of 'God' as 'the word which became a *name*'. This emphasis reveals the weakness of 'name' as a characterization of 'God'. Rather than a name, 'God' is a title for something to which we do not give a name, not comprehending it sufficiently to identify it. We give it the title 'God' as to say 'Unknown Thing of the highest order of being!' and with the title make appeal to it to give us our reality, which it seems to hold in its own. But, not knowing what its reality is, we do not know what it is that we ask — or what response is made, or if there be a response given. This ignorance-baffled intercourse Martin Buber splits metaphysically into a 'dialogue' — a pompous word that has become intellectually fashionable with the assistance of his special use of it. In a 'dialogue' relationship, the other than I is often but a puppet of I's egocentric notioning; and, in much of the human vis-à-vis with 'God' of contemporary religious metaphysics, the interlocution follows this pattern — it is a gymnastics of which the other is the theoretical inspiration, but the object of which is benefit for the human actor. — But I have no reproach for the notion of God as the notion of the spirit in its immensity not known as (though abstractly titled as) single, yet of which we feel that we must so know it and can only so know it. I have no reproach for our ignorance of the spirit as the reality of being, as One pervading being. Knowledge of the spirit as of a thing-by-itself is not to be expected; to know it we must know far, expansively, and in tried continualness. The wrong in the notion of God is a wrong in the notion of ourselves: in the notion of God there is an ignorance of ourselves. And I have the immediate reproach as to this to ourselves that we, now, addressing ourselves to varying blackboard activities of self-knowing, analyse ourselves into non-self-resemblance, and have no other blackboard subject besides these stranger-ourselves but a Stranger called titlelessly 'Existence'.

Spinoza, a religious dialectician of a different mood from Buber's, shows how close to truth the notion of God can be brought. The human thinking into the divine and the divine thinking into the human, he nearly makes one notion: the dichotomy 'human' and 'divine' seems in his mind's management almost a technical differentiation. But, afraid to err, he stanches the imagination of ourselves, believing in us through believing in God. Spinoza's notion is a tortuously virtuous unity of knowledge and ignorance; it stands the human on the brink of itself in a purity of self-suspicion.

9 · passage 23

I speak in this passage only of Freud. There are other scientists of the mind who have squeezed the reality of intelligent being — the account of its nature — into frames of interpretation constructed, as is the Freudian, not according to available knowledge of the mind's functioning in its essential character, as the intelligence, and at its most active, articulate, self-expressive, in the rational continuities of thought, but according to supposed clues from *outside* the field of its characteristic, i.e., intelligent, functioning. The frames of interpretation used by all the pioneer modern psychologists were made to fit emotional behavior manifesting itself in disruptions of the life of the intelligence, on the assumption that in this behavior lie the elementary conditions, the rudimentary laws, of mental life. Freud supplied the basic proposition that the *non-thinking*, the intellectually uncollected and undigested, merely reactive, phases of being-behavior constitute the primary human mind. The other human-mind analysers have embroidered this basic proposition with refinements that bestow upon these raw phases a significance of implicit intelligence. The entire content of the human intelligence has been transposed from its natural mental setting of personal self-familiarity and cultural educatedness in itself to the physical, or, rather, the physiological, setting of human existence, in the theories as to the nature of the human mind in which Freud's fellows in the scientific appropriation of the subject have attempted to improve, with various elegant qualifications, his rough, crude conception of human truth as resident in archetypal physiological mentality. — One has in Freud the germ of the modern religion of psychology, the gospel sense of which is that in the beginning Body created the mind and the intelligence. More elevated or sophisticated versions of the doctrine do not transcend the grim materialistic levels of its mythology of mental origins.

I shall just cite the Jungian version of the Freudian doctrine. In this attempt to beautify the grim Freudian picture of the 'unconscious' as the physiological matrix of the mind, the concept of the elementarily unintelligent human mental individual, human self, is dignified by the suggestion that the existent all-else extends from it in a grand unity of sub-intelligent identity with it, the self being thus enlarged with the substance of the material universal environment, capable of functioning as its artistic unconscious by putting faculties of *intelligence* to the task. There could be no such irrational playing with the fire of physiological romanticism if the speculation was not secured to the basic realistic concept, which, indeed, posits a basic mental condition of common-place, 'natural', insanity. The attractions of the Jungian improvements on the concept are those of a higher insanity.

10 · passages 24, 27, 28, 29

". . . one-being mounts to emergence from the ordeal of Difference called 'the universe' . . ." *(24)* ". . . that rounding-in and exhaustion of diversity which is human. Thus from physicality emerge persons — ourselves." *(28)* The point of my making these quotations concerns the words 'emergence' and 'emerge'. But I see a need of my commenting on 'from physicality emerge persons — ourselves' incidentally, and at once. This must not be detached from its context; detached, it would seem to account for human nature as a product of physical nature, but such is not its sense. 'Physicality' here is not Initial Reality. It is of a contingent nature, resulting from an event-like development in initial reality — which, by my account of human nature, is the Ancestor (that comes along!). The first quotation can be made use of here as a guardian of the sense of the second.

The words 'emergence' and 'emerge' of the quotations are intended to express a sense of process: they are used not just in report of an occurrence of an emerging, but with connotation of a sequence — a graduated occurrence — reaching its term at a point of issuance. My use of these words may remind some of the phenomenon of emergence, the idea of an emerging, that Teilhard de Chardin stressed in his account of a 'personal universe'.

Now, while, before writing *The Telling*, I had some acquaintance with philosophy, this amounted, on the whole, to a spare knowledge; I have felt no special devotion of mind to it, nor have I been in any relation of intellectual kinship with it in a general or any particular respect. After the writing of *The Telling* I have looked with a little extra closeness, here and there, at specializedly philosophical and religious writings in which there was treating of subjects and questions of some relatedness to those on which I speak in *The Telling*. This I have not done with the attitude of a disputing or concurring colleague to their authors, for on what I speak I speak from direct personal interest without circumscriptions of professional philosophic or professional or categorical religious interest, but to gauge my words' aptness to my always differing principle of treatment, and trend of meaning, *and* to educate myself for possible needs of explaining differences between my and others' modes of thought and word where there seemed not only parallelism but convergence of idea. I should not counter all pointing to sameness of words between my own and others' expression with a fierce and flat all-covering claim of that brand of intellectual private property called 'originality'. We all use words more or less the same in being centered to the actuality of human nature and identity set in a recognized comprehensive circumstance, and are naturally and properly subject to having our words meet in coincidences resulting from our having concerns of thought necessarily more or less the same — to the degree to which we exercise our humanity in thought.

There could be pointing to words of mine as expressive, for instance, of concepts of Platonic or neo-Platonic origin. I should acknowledge co-incidences. I should not place 'originality' in the antique instances; I should argue, from my own experience of autochthonous sponsoring of words, the general human circumstance of thought-engagement in subjects ultimately of a common character — *as* we think. My focus of argument would be, where comparison was focused on resemblances, on *differences*: for what I say in and with the words is free of all doctrinaire philosophical or religious association, is of spontaneous generation, and what value it may have proceeds from this. To specify, in example. If I speak of 'Good' or speak of 'One' or The One, I do so under no influence of suggestion of the word or the concept from any other — the words are mine without any reference of consciousness in their use of their being any others'. With respect to the writings of Plotinus, in which the concept of The One is dominative, I have to say that I had not read them before the composition of *The Telling*. I should add that, while Plotinus inherited this concept from the Semitic Philo, The One for me does not reside in the conceptual domain; in speaking of this I am speaking of some-'thing' encountered in the domain of my personal knowledge-experience, as of a reality that requires no intellectual deduction or confirmation (but not spurning the processes of verification that the intellectual conscience calls for, for human good-faith, and honor).

Specifically, as to the utterances of Teilhard de Chardin (which, as I have indicated, I had not met with when I conceived, and wrote, *The Telling*): his sensitivity to the moving, in the reality of human existence, of the meaning of Being in a determinative way had the obstruction in it of theological concepts. "In the final reckoning, above Man's rediscovered grandeur . . . there reappears — not doing violence to but preserving the integrity of Science — in our universe seen through the most modern eyes, the face of God." Over and over, his perception [the terms I use are mine] of the working, in the existence of the physical universe and that of human beings in their aspect as beings conscious of Being, of a resolving-process directed towards a culmination of the entire manifestation of the phenomena of Being in a comprehensive *Definition* is blanked out, all the sensitivity immanent in it neutralized, by the imposition of the theologically decreed 'God-the-Creator' conception as the ultimate ruling logic of final definition. Theological obedience causes him to lose the meanings of his perception of the progressive actuality of Being in anticipations of Being as ultimately defined in reiterative terms. As: "The task of the world consists in . . . consummating itself through union with a pre-existing Being." His preoccupation with, and love of, science and linking of religious faith with faith in the scientific doctrine of evolution, while responding to his intuitions of the permeation of the totality of the Existent with meaning as an ultimately plain, defined unity because science seems to define at least the physical aspects of Being in a way prophetic of ultimate definition, trapped his intuitions in the endless summations of science, which are incapable, by its nature, of doing more than partially define (and partial definition cannot but be in some way in error).

For all his great, his spiritually wide-cast sensitivity, Teilhard de Chardin had, yet, it might be said, nowhere to go, no staying-place: it drove him back and forth between scientific and theological retreats, and confusions speak out of the transit. Thus, the theologically strict God-the-Creator, the 'pre-existing Being' conception, is countered with a conception of 'God the eternal being in himself' who "is everywhere, we might say, in process of formation in us." (It may be helpful for readers of *The Telling* for me to depose here that my conception of the spiritual history of the phenomena of existence, in which the human existence-manifestation is seen standing up amidst them not adding to the phenomenal existence-quantity, but bringing it to a head of unity of reference to a universal order of meaning, involves no reversion to 'a' pre-existing Being as a reiterative ultimate of experienceable reality, or evolutionary interpretation of human existence as reiterating in itself the eternal existence of a divine being in formative terms. Perhaps the simplest key to the differences between de Chardin's and my conceptions is in the fact that the spiritual history that I outline does not have, as its crowning end, its beginning, in glorifying revelation. Such spiritual history is essentially static — its evolutionary scientific liberalism has some movement in it, but to no consequence, being but an exercise in intellectual freedom clamped between poles of dogma.)

Teilhard de Chardin looked to his notion of 'the cosmic Christ' to dissipate the confusions and contradictions of his theory of a universe absorbed in the grandeur of a divine nature. Christ, by his notions, divinizes humanity — in which the universe has evolutionarily reached 'hominization': Christ is the center-point of intermediation between the divine and the non-divine, where the universe emerges as a universe in which spirit has primacy. The point is a point of accumulation of "a Consciousness and a Personalization" in the universe "that is continually growing greater — an exact reversal of the World of modern science". Here begins the understanding of "the Personality of God and the immortality of the soul as elements essential to the structure of my universe" — which is "a World that is quite certainly open at its summit in *Christo Jesu*".

The differences between such a story as de Chardin's of 'emergence' and my own of *The Telling* can be described perhaps most economically in terms of the kind of source we presumed for our story-matière. His matière consists of a number of stories. His story is a synthesis of 'historically important' varieties of story-matter. (I do not hesitate to categorize the material of science thus — meaning by the phrase, important relatively to a period of time as an organizing of thought-tendencies dominant in it into a definition that serves as an accepted 'truth', or story-apparatus, in the time, a common area of mental pause, emotional agreement.) His passionate dedication of himself to discovery of the yet undiscovered essentialities in which inhere the meaning of the existence of a World was weighted against itself from the start of his quest by the heavy load of historical story-equipment with which he set out. He sought to transcend the sense of his stories with the help of their collective sense. His stories were, a philosophically historicized theological religion, an adamant legacy of many periods of time, and a Christianity, a durable theological narrative, become latterly faint in its personal, literal, story-force, energized with a modern metaphysics of spirituality as physically concentrated in and disseminated out through Christ, *and* science as a narrative of materiality wanting but filling out and completing with the anticipatory tale of the spiritual maturation of materiality. No such sense-transcendence of all this as he imagined was possible. He succeeded only in making a historical synthesis of 'truth' formulations that lent to his intuitions of the Essentialities a modern appearance of historicity in his eyes, while swallowing them into itself. — I have placed the source, in *The Telling*, *in* the human reality of the teller: knowledge for the telling comes, in my book, from the direct access that humanness of being provides to Intelligent Acquaintance with Being, as the story-ground of truth. I see such a one as de Chardin as a devotee of truth whose canons of truth immediately, on his assuming the rôle of teller, caused him to lose his way, and himself, in history, which he desperately tried to bring spiritually up to date.

I ought to be more specific as to how The One of my evocation differs from The One of Plotinus' postulation. An account of the difference is anticipated in the words 'evocation' and 'postulation'. These express my sense of the difference between the experiences inspiring the use of the titular phrase. Plotinus presented The One as a subject of necessary beliefs, an intellectual postulate the verification of the reality of which must be left to mystical knowledge-experience. In my presentation, The One is not at the distance of abstraction, to be endowed with human meaning by a mixture of speculation and contemplation; not a source and a term of all being that transcends being *and* knowing. I speak of that which one knows in knowing oneself as a speaker of the reality of Being, and of the reality of one's being, in the speaking, and even of the reality of the speaking. One does not, in this, speak of The One as the Idea of ideas, an indefinable ultimate of definition. The *idea* of it, for me, is but the antique obscurity that envelops it. The obscurity thickens in later, and later, times, as human individuality becomes the increasingly dominant subject of intellectual preoccupation, or idea — oneness made a distributed phenomenon, with various theoretical collectivisms employing human individuality as a rational basis of generalization to replace the old religio-philosophic Idea-of-ideas Oneness.

The One, for me, is a One that each full human being 'comes up against' — to speak as of a close physical encounter — in being that: human being truly lived is lived close up to the inevitable manifestation of a living all-comprehensive reality of Being's One-being to the human one. The encounter is not a mystery, of which only contemplation can make report, an event futurized in an impossibility of immediate access to its actuality. It has immediate actuality in our speaking. It and we are of one time, of one utterance in our speaking; our speaking speaks the actuality. The human one, by fidelity to the word-making unities of its being, by which it is human, and the One that is Being's fidelity to its truth-spirited unity with all itself, meet in a connateness of little and great by an equality of the spirit. Thus do I, meaning with regard to The One as I have described, speak of 'evocation', to express my meaning. The One, for me, is ever-present to our *evocation*. For Plotinus, The One is outside of cognizance, removed from encounter — a non-intellectual postulate of the intellect: one might describe such a religious idea of human realization of a sense of cosmicality as an intellectually induced inebriation.

The word 'inebriation' is exact to Plotinus' conception. I mean no mockery of him, with it, or with anything else I say of him. Indeed, having come to know (somewhat) how Plotinus labored to integrate reason and the personal sense of cosmicality (spurred by Philo's forceful injection of religious conceptions of unity into the philosophic), I reflect sadly on how those, of 'liberated' religiosity, of the latest generations, wandering in loose search of a port, have not by kind accident come to rest for a while at Plotinus — or Teilhard de Chardin. They would, at least, with these, be introduced to their intellects as part of themselves innately possessed, and not the creation of the winds and spindrift of that world-talk that goes round and round, the spill of the intellectual confusions of ages invading minds as emptinesses inviting substance. Spinoza would make them a fine harbor for a while of healthful ministration to their minds without home. But he offers few amenities. Those other two are softer. But I make no recommendations. I mean no more than that the wanderers could have done better for their minds than they have done.

To stay a little longer with Plotinus, and questions of differences between his description of the human relationship to cosmic reality, as all, One, and named The One, and his understanding of the human reality, and mine. There is a comparability in the provision for cosmic occurrence in which the human and the One attain to a perfect unity of reality. For Plotinus this is a return of the human soul to the One. The soul, for me, is not of primordial existence: 'return' is not applicable. Nor is the One a primordially existent identity remaining itself namably in the constancy of universal continuity. Reunion is, for me, the *knowing*, gathered together in human being, of the one-nature of being *given up to*, delivered into the keeping of, Being; and the primordially existent identity is Soul. Soul, the primordial state of Being, in which is all, yields for a reason to a state of All, in which will be found One. My presentation does not omit the trouble that overtook the All-Soul, within itself — even because of its being all. I call it 'trouble' in a domestic-spirited fondness for all this difficulty of a universal state in which we, human, have had to labor to be in order to know, so that Being might be proved to itself good, indivisible — of a beneficent indivisibleness. The trouble *is* this difficulty of a universal state, and it is also a necessity of Being, ordained to itself, the reason of our being, our having come to be, of the succeeding, to undifferentiated Soul, of differentiation. And we are souls by our labor of being issuing in knowing, and our knowing well enough to speak well enough to one another the message of Being to itself by which its identity will inform it under the name of One, and the first reality, Soul, take life in it as the blessing of the One on our late reality of souls.

Plotinus' pattern of understanding beguiles. Likewise, the Platonic pattern beguiles. (One can read, in Plotinus, efforts to loosen and enlarge the Platonic pattern with the less capricious, more soberly religious thinking that Philo contributed to the philosophic canon.) — Even, what I am here, in this note, presenting may beguile — please an interest of readers, in the subjects on which I comment, of a specialized kind. But

I mean no departure here from my sense of my relation to readers underlying *The Telling* itself, which is for me a relation of myself, in my speaking, to their human persons, and not a relation of myself to philosophic persons, or persons by intellectual class religious. While favoring here somewhat propensities readers may have towards wandering from the relation I attempt to make in *The Telling* proper between myself, my words, and themselves, their personal attention, my idea has been to do no more wandering myself than what respect for their objectivity seems to call for, the standing off for the narrowed look that distances, to bring other matter into the picture, bearings of judgement's proper cautions — and for the ears' pondering the question "Have we not heard all this before?"

11 · passage 27 (further)

The theme of contrariety — 'how Being could in ways go counter to itself' — into which I look in this passage I came to by my own path of thought, without the aid of the direction-sign of any other. But, since the writing of it, I have met with other thought at the meeting-place of the subject; and, surely, it is a natural meeting-place, this subject close in simplicity to the very first subjects, those of the very first degree of simplicity. Jacob Boehme, I found, had written: "Nothing without contrariety can become manifest to itself: for, if it has nothing to resist it, it goes eventually of itself outwards, and returns not again into itself. But if it return not into itself, as into that out of which it originally went, it knows nothing of its primal being." And this is indeed a strong argument. But, too much of the nature of an argument; it lacks sympathetic insight into the nature of contrariety's necessity. It is not the necessity of 'everything', everything of a multifarious All of being, general being, but a necessity of Being as a thing of *one* integrity; nor, necessary for the protection of its existence, or its existence to itself in the knowledge of itself, but necessary by mere necessity of its nature as self-justifying, careful of itself, and of its love of what it is — a most generous subjection of itself in all its possibilities to Criticism.

One could apply with more literal truth-force to the work-ings of a universal criticism in the universe of Being, than to the theological setting of its truistic pronouncement on the critical potency of scripture, the Pauline formula on a Criticism centered in contrarieties as naturally existent to the point of Criticism itself's being naturally existent; so that, one might say, "All anticipating, in the one-natured conscience of Being, of wrong being that might take being 'is given by inspiration' — Being self-inspired with care without limit for its entire perfection — 'and is profitable for doctrine' — a custom of principle of Being's own making, for Being's follow-ing — and 'for reproof, for correction, for instruction in righteousness.'" Or, to simplify this depiction of what I have named Criticism: the discipline, and the knowledge, admini-stered *with* being, in Being's one-conscienced, unlimitedly just inspiration of being.

I found — one finds — this question of contrariety em-braced in Spinoza's account of the totality of things in the consideration of the question of perfection. In Being, or Being as God, with God its comprehensive identity in its utter totality, there is, can be, no imperfection because there could be no alternative to the total creation: this — Spinoza's *natura naturata* — must be regarded as perfect, the natural issue of there being "that which is in itself and conceived through itself, or those attributes of substance which express eternal and infinite essence, that is to say, God in so far as He is considered as a free cause" — which Spinoza distinguished as *natura naturans*. In other words, the nature of Being includes all possibilities of being by its very perfectness. There is a purposive absence of moralism, a fear of applying mere moralism, in Spinoza's dealing with the subject of Being as the original and ultimate Real, the unconditioned to which all things existent in difference by its totality-implying nature are relative. The question of wrong, of flaw, of contrariety, cannot arise in Spinoza because he will not discuss Being as relative to that which is *of* it, is a derivative of its nature: his conception of the 'free cause' of all is of such a purity that he will not include in it anything suggestive of judgement of it as productive in its causal existence of right, wrong, good, bad — anything that would make contradiction an attribute of it, and thus deny its existence in denying its perfectness. Even, Spinoza protects his conception of perfection as, simply, the necessary perfection of the nature of Being, by a refusal to identify it as Good: this would relativize it — subject it to the relativistic modes of human judgement.

Spinoza was trying to liberate the conception of God, in his time, from notions attributing this and that particular manifestation or anticipation to 'the will of God' — to defend the utter *moral* disinterestedness of essential Being, its perfect conscience prescribing that nothing of what might be existent by it be suppressed. This makes for a removal of Being from identification with the processes of *Time*, and, even, with the *processes* of creation itself; it establishes Being, rightly, in its ultimate, its unaffectable, realness as one with itself. But if the intermediate identification of Being with the processes of time is excluded from consideration, the sequel to time is but as if a return of Being to itself as it was in a primal state of quiescent self-indetermination: 'everything' has happened, but it is as if nothing has happened — nothing is 'really' different from how it was 'in the beginning'. But the very processes of time belong to a difference-in-the-making between 'first' and ultimate, by reason of creation. And the difference has to do with the inevitability, by the natural presence in the universe of Being, of processes of judgement giving everything (perfect) trial of (perfect) compatibility with the (perfect) nature of being: adjudication between contrariety-in-totality and totality-as-one is a universal motive, and time an expression of it.

I see Spinoza as defining things in terms of the primeval eternal, which takes only so far as the end of the Age of Creation. I try to stand us on a ground of sense of that eternal which is Being's continuity graduated from the temporal infinity of universal variation into the infinity of sameness of being with itself proved to itself in the being of ourselves as time-wise numbers that tell of One. Said Spinoza, answering the challenge, why so many imperfections in Nature: "Because to Him material was not wanting for the creation of everything, from the highest to *the very lowest grade of perfection* [italics, mine!]; or, to speak more properly, because the laws of his nature were so ample that they sufficed for the production of everything which can be conceived by an infinite intellect." The possibility, so clearly demonstrated here, of evasion by a sternly rational mind of recognition of the existence of contrariety in the total corpus of being, comes of Spinoza's confining himself to telling the story of Being and Beings by, only, defining the characters of the story. This, so far as it goes, is but a *dramatis personae* presentation. It has been, still must be, wondrously refreshing to minds become jaded in following the zealously circumstantial involutions of professional religious narratives of what has been, is and will be going on, universally. But, not marking a difference between the definition of the characters and the presenting of the action and interaction of the story in which they are characters, Spinoza allows himself to make his definition of the characters sufficient as story of the action and interaction. This scrupulosity of concentration on the establishing of the characters in sharp outlines of ineluctable distinction (for which there is much to be said, as against both traditional and anti-traditional sentimental play with cloudily conceived unities of distinguished divine and human identities) tends to immobilize the characters themselves in parts imperfectly life-like, being-like.

12 · passages 32, 40, 41, 57

". . . for natural rings the fervor of devotion to what fills the place of truth." I am moved to append some observations on the variety of religious provisions that human beings have had presented to them for their spiritual comfort — or shall we better say, spiritual sanity — in their travelling through, in, across, time's interminable-seeming extensions of itself. It is not generally perceived that the desire for something different in belief-formulation among those who, mainly the younger of us, now refuse the scheduled choices of such travel-accommodations is powered by the energy of self-interest, without the encumbrance of the older admixture of desire for truth, with the desire for comfort. This new 'religious' preoccupation is therefore far less confused, more susceptible of independent individual management, than the older. It can seem unconventionally religious while being not religious at all. It is, on the whole, mere neurological therapeutics. I say 'neurological' rather than 'psychological' just because it is concerned with the treatment of spiritual 'nervousness' — this is a verbal vulgarism, but an appropriate one here, the condition, in so far as it is identified with religious preoccupation, being itself a classificatory vulgarism.

How much of the Oriental religious positions, doctrines, prescriptions, that made their way into the religious emptiness of so many contemporary minds has nothing to do with religion, is not concerned with the things of religion but with therapies aimed at the spiritual nerves? It is their being predominantly concerned with these therapies that has earned them the hospitality of these minds, and made them the bolstering reading-matter, the recipe-books for peace-of-mind, of the young and others who, expressing a weariness, mounted in human hope, of waiting for a religion all of truth, strike this truth-objective from the spiritual schedule. The journey becomes its own objective, 'feeling good' in the making of the journey becomes the standard of spiritual value. Spirituality is

166

despiritualized. Religion has its truth-dedication extracted from it — its claws of sharp wishing to tell the rightly believable pulled out. The new-style believers (and we must not forget the influence of science's simplification of the notion of truth, in its seeming to explode truth into an infinity of infinitesimally small self-verifying statements, which continually gather into innumerable varying impermanent truths to the continual nullification of the possibility of an integral truth) seek, rather than religious documentation, literature from which to imbibe ideas of how to keep from being harassed by the possession of a spiritual nature (how to make it, rather than themselves, as it were, behave!). Their Oriental lesson-texts are of literary not scriptural reality for them. Actual novels (for instance, those of Herman Hesse) serve as their idea-sources of spiritual postures that will not hurt, tire, but bestow even a sense of worldly ease, or, at least, of worldly sang-froid. The novel, indeed, has long been developing into the lay text-book of post-religious religiosity — each on each's spiritual own — so far as it may be possible to follow and yet not follow the novelist's attitudes to the characters' behavior or what the behavior itself suggests — that is, a main sacredness attaches here to caprice itself.

The contemporary rôle of the novel as a mode of suggesting spiritual positions utterly free from the kind of preoccupation that made religion loved (the wish to make itself true) is well-covered in a long article in *The Times Literary Supplement* of June 6, 1971, in which the novels of James Hanley are the subject of comprehensive praise. A reviewer of one of his early novels is chided for having thought the story to have 'universal significance', to which view I think I do no injustice in assuming it to imply an authorial deference to an over-all human objective of truth on a religious scale. The contemporary-period critic of this novelist's work rejects this view indignantly as a misrepresentation of the author's spiritual position, which he describes as anti-ideological, associating the ideological in spiritual position with that category of easiest intellectual snobbery, become a catch-all of opprobrious characterization: 'middle-class'. The 'logic' — presumably, therapeutic value as distinguished from ideological or truth-related value — of this novelist's 'creative vision' is, in the later reviewer's liberated critical language, a "vision of the importance to a person of the right to live his own life in whatever way suits and satisfies him, however wrong, or disgraceful, it might look or sound to others." Here we have a very thorough tracking, down to its essential spiritual scope, of the new function of literature as anti-scripture to the scriptural. (I do not bring poets into this picture: I consider poets in the late-modern era to have converted poetry into a *lingua franca* of exhibitionism, an exhibitionism of many types having a common character of removing distinctions between affectation and sincerity — poetry seems to me to have been reduced to verbal theatrics and separated from its identity as literature's fountain-head of spiritual seriousness.)

Is it not a deep-reaching and far-extending and essentially characteristic peculiarity of the Oriental religious preoccupation that emphasis is on the therapy of spiritual composure, with the matter of truth total — the story of our being, and Being, that will embrace us in the fulness of its utterance — a shadow all-attendant on the figure of self-questioning life but never part of it? And the corresponding peculiarity of West-ward forms of spiritual behavior-expression, of management of the excitation and disturbance of consciousness that insistencies of soul in human nature produce: is not emphasis *here* on the truth-aspect of the spiritual objective, the knowing of the Whole, the being told, or telling, it? It is this difference that makes the Oriental administration of words *literature*, inherently, and the Westward administration of words *scripture*! — and explains in considerable part the attraction of the Oriental to the spiritually excited irreligiosity with which so many 'Western' contemporary minds are affected. Oriental religious storying is literary, not scriptural. But the Westward religious storying, the great trends in it of address as to the human audience entire, the Hebraic and Christian religious outsweeping of words, is travestied if treated, used, as literature. It seems to me that the Moslem is, in kind, in these terms, a mixture of scripture and literature.

The magnetism of the religious personality of Jesus is in his bringing this matter of the Whole Story to a Crux: *it must be told*, it must not be put off, and put off, as it is in ritual. Not just put off, put off, is the Story, in all that is no more than literature: it is changed. There, questions of soul are treated of as private nervosities, either in a grand style, of spiritual color, or in the matter-of-fact black, white, and shading of secular concentration on the human self as the theme of the Story. An aggregate story is formed of the stories of human lives, sometimes framed in religious sentiment, having defined or implicit religious reference, sometimes not. This is a supposititious Whole Story, the very principle of which is, Fiction. The actuality cannot be other than one story made of the story of Being and the story of the stories of human beings, and by none of the distributed sympathies that produce literature, but by a necessity of telling Unity. The necessity is sympathy undivided, urging the story of All — gathering, gathering, in us (this our humanness) — to go forth from us, be truth, be one. None was ever so closely wrapped, so tightly caught, within the enfolding sympathy that urges the one story to go forth to its telling as was Jesus.

Jesus felt that compulsive sympathy as a command from — what the difference between himself and the source of the command? All the humiliating anguish of human uncertainty and the companion pride of human certainty, are pressed together in his joining of the identities of a commander will and a commanded willingness in himself, and in his offering himself as both the teller and the embodiment of the Whole

Story. That is, he attempted an immediate delivery of a story that would prove to be the unified large of truth — *the* story — in an eternal telling by him, the eternal being *of* him. This tremendous act of attempting to force truth forth for everyone's relief from spiritual ignorance by anticipating the consequences of knowledge — it is not merely historical stuff of scripture, it is a scriptural act. One might say, he tried to give religion fulfilment of its truth-objective by trying to create truth out of himself. I wrote once, in a poem, that "he signed his name to a tale by us/To be written." I think this looks towards what I mean in my description, here: Jesus' possessedness with a necessity working in him as one who could not endure that the Story — the One Story — should go for more human whiles veiled in priestly obscurities. A breach in time there seemed to him to be, to fill; and he gave himself to the filling of it with himself — as if time could be mended, and become at once our measure of life-eternal.

The scriptural act of Jesus reminds how we are not yet, and not yet, telling what waits for us to tell one another; how we wait — hidden from one another in time, which silences one moment, one day, with the next, one hour's or year's speaking, by any, with the next hour's, or the next year's — to prove ourselves capable of telling it. This reminds, falls in with a continually renewed reproach we make of ourselves for living by passing words, as if there could be temporary truths — a reproach hidden from ourselves. The 'religious life', which some still in part live, resounds with reminders of a Story-to-tell, that, seeming the voice of truth evoking truth, seem to bring the very Story within the reach of spiritual hearing. But more and more the spiritual life of human beings is the literary life: more and more human beings lose the truth-zest that only *one* Story as the Story of all can satisfy, and commit themselves to the care of literature — the ministrations of *stories* (coming from all the existent modes and quarters of invention in the name of public interest and benefit, in teeming provision). There is a character of story-of-stories, or relationship to the concepts of literary pluralism within the terms of which people now in large proportion pursue their lives, in very much that is now put forth not directly as story, but as wisdom of human life as a diversity of human numbers, a vari-storied populace whose unity is in a legislative intelligence of itself as a plurality without intrinsic unity.

The pattern I have sketchily drawn of the general disposing of human spirituality between religious and literary forms of expression and definition could be strengthened with historical particularization and filled in with illustrative matter, especially with respect to the late-modern temper of human spirituality, to some persuasive effect, I think. For instance, Marxian political philosophy, and the philosophical trends characterizable as 'existentialist', and many trends in late-modern psychology, psycho-analysis, and the biological-anthropological sciences, are reasonably viewable as belonging, in varying degree but none less than markedly so, to literature as a category of human dealing with spiritual problems, in the sense I have described. The breaking-down of the scriptural concept of story into more and more individualized personal-story units — even, in some developments, to the loss of unity of the story-form itself; the paralleling of natural animal self-particularizing to a limited real personal environment and the abnormal tendency in a human self to withdraw into an unreal 'world of its own'; this force of disintegration of the human identity into personal particles, each its own story or part of an isolated story — with only scientific systems to hold loosely assembled story-facts in historical poise; — this is the end of a course of a separation of the pursuit of the truth-objective into the religious and the literary mode of spiritual narrative. The one was faithful to the one-story nature of truth. The other, the literary, was faithful to human nature, in the difficulty of pursuing the objective: where religion was arbitrary, telling one small story over and over, and ever asking belief, rather than telling more and more, literature was lenient, asking no belief, and telling more and more, and ever more differently than could be true, in all.

I am moved to linger with the idea of literature I have been presenting, having some thought to communicate that I think may be useful on that element of literature which is actually of the stuff of stories. This concerns the story-writing of the Russians, the influence of which has penetrated far into 'Western' story-making. In their stories, the human being is stripped to naked individuality; each one is, oh, so vividly, but, oh, so constrictedly, present in the two dimensions of being-self and being not-the-other. There can, within these limits, be active play of sensibility, and of spiritual feeling, but there is no spiritual dimension. The narrative honesty is truth stripped to a bare secularity. All the burden of truth in its magnificence of spiritual entirety is elsewhere — the stories, however grim or sad in substance, are not oppressed by it, have a lightness, as if by a general agreement that what relates to mere human beings, while very important from their point of view, is, in considerations lying outside the boundaries of their lives, that is, from the point of view best describable in this context as lofty, not very important, if important at all. This lowliness of the story-level of human characterization makes everyone feel at home. It seems all so simple, what a human being is seems so patent: humanity is seen as existing in a cage of the fact of it, a great cage of all-inclusive humanness, every individual a type, every type a caged infinity. This objectivism has infiltrated modern storying forcefully — it being an emotional objectivism, the story-tellers putting themselves imaginatively inside the cage with the creatures — because of the weakening in 'Western' literature, in its total secularization, its divorcement of the human being from the religion-nursed one-story concept of existence, and of truth, of the concept of the human being itself.

The Russians extracted the brute fact of human existence from the pre-modern loose alliance of religion and literature in a mystical credo of having the same story-content, and with this they relieved modern-literature secularity of its emptiness of human beings as creatures of some dignity of bonafide identity. The identity enjoyed by human beings under other dispensations had had at least the dignity of association with ideas of the spirituality of human nature, though these did not comprise usefully comprehensible definition of it. The human being of modern-literature secularity became increasingly an abstraction, a dismal one, to be enlivened with the personal play upon it of aesthetics, and scientific and philosophical lending to it of objectively appreciable significances. With the Russian contribution of the mere but actual human being, the story-character of human beings, which had been breaking up into nothingness in this secularity, had some flesh put into it. Flesh in its cheerful varieties, but not spirit: the relief of the dismalness does not extend to the spiritual nothingness of the human being in the modern-literary abstract.

There is another side to the episode of Russian contribution to 'Western' modernism: the Russian political-philosophical contribution of an ideology (however non-Russian its intellectual sources, the vitality that practicalized it is distinctly Russian) that throws out the necessity of an elusive spiritual commanding force, the One-Truth, One-Story urgency, and puts solidly in its place a necessity of unmistakable and undisregardable commandingness, the urgency of truth as a composite idea derived from history, a mandate of interpretations of the human past by which human beings are to know themselves as what they are collectively in the present, actually and potentially, in terms of deductions from history of what they were collectively in the past. This objectivist practicality puts *something* 'there', where spiritual necessity, moving in human beings, made do with religious or literary models or imperatives or combinations of these, but now seems to have only the choice between the old, truth by habit of belief, with fainter, fainter, pleasure-taking in the sentiment of truth, and freakish new truth-ordinances, that cannot exert authority long enough to become habit — and nothing. And thus, in its modern poverty of equipment and vigor for the (oh, short) rest of the spiritual journey to its truth-end, has much of humanity ('the human world') fed on a fare of Russian prescription.

Should one rejoice that, because of the Russian contribution to modern literature, the stuff of story is more of flesh than of abstract make-up? Would it have been better for the story-public to know the actual spiritual starvation it suffered, and not indulge its literary appetite in this long stop-over in the cosmopolis of the infinitely multiple 'mere' human being? And should one thank the Russians for the provision of this distillation, this potion that, distilled from history and given the name of truth, goes fast to the brains of weary travellers, and energizes them with argument-stimuli suggesting that the journey is over — except for some arrangements of proving, persuading, and warning, that it *is* over? Human beings are indeed weary — how long this journey has been going on! It ought to be over. We ought by now to be reaching the end, to be at the end — and getting out of the train, the vehicle, the vehicles, carrying us across the borders of one uncertainty and into and out of another, and so on, and on. But to declare thus that an end is reached, to administer, and to imbibe, this intoxicant that converts history into eschatology, makes the soul the dupe of the brain.

What I have been just now speaking of has affected learned heads, confused and worried heads, drooping heads, defiant heads, unlearned heads, all kinds of heads, in uniform ways. They become filled with a confidence very difficult to match or exceed in firmness: it is, assurance that history corroborates them. There seems to be no *sagacious* countering of this with something else. Those who would like to offer something else, in sagacity, but do not go mentally armed with a counter-assurance, keep warily at a diffident distance. Who is sure enough of anything to counter with it what has the authority of history behind it — or the spirit of history, which is the same thing?

What has history at its back has history before it: sureness resting on history is the sureness of those who lock themselves, and others with them, in historical 'truth', a self-consuming story — it ages in the telling, it has begun to end with its beginning.

We have had so much, ever, where we lacked that it was, ever, difficult to know what lacked, to see what it was that we had not. Now, when what we had thins in many places, increasingly, and we can see through to past actualities of not having had in what we had what we thought we had, or as much as we thought we had, we begin to know what we are without, and to know well the nature of everything that minimizes the extent of the lack and compensates for it with what does not answer to it: such is the preliminary sureness that suffices finally. For, as we know this — and it takes only the calm of final non-disillusionment to know it, for that we want to have ourselves gathered in story was never illusion, whatever else was — we shall provide ourselves with what we are without, have ever been without, in the measure of happiness in the knowledge. To know what we have to do, to give ourselves, though in the midst of sore consequence of its not having been done, not having been given, is pure hope, which heals the wounds of failure.

This long note — a complex of comments — in which I have spoken so much in terms of 'the story', 'the one story', stories, would not be complete without some words concerning my use of this language, itself. The conception that I have here dwelt on, in outright formulation, statement and restatement, in thematic expansion, in concentrated literalness of sense, centered in the idea of there being a story to tell, to tell which gives *truth*, a one story that tells all there is to tell, in unity, according to its unity — this conception I formed long ago, speaking it in the beginning with a convinced simplicity, without elaborated awareness of all its implications, in its breadth. The simple pronouncement became as it were a key to articulate knowledge of much that I foreknew. I spoke the conception to intimates, to share the pleasure I felt in it as a natural secret that had yielded itself up to me — for telling. It can be found in my earlier writings, in formulative variations, and as a motif of thought everywhere in my recorded thought. It is, of course, a prominent motif of thought and expression in *The Telling* itself.

I did not know till a few years ago, a number of years after the writing of *The Telling*, that someone had made free to take possession of this motif and, treating it as new literary property, used it to strike a note and attitude of simple spontaneity of wisdom for a single small composition. I learned of this from an academic study in which adoptions of a related sort, not all unknown to me, as this one was, were cited. I have since occasionally had it brought to mind. But not until I was well forward in this note did the fact make appearance to me, as an interloper between my thought, my formulation, my theme of the one story, and myself. I have been exorcising this interloper, therefore, in every reminding presence of it to my progress in this note. And I mean, in touching on the matter here, also to exorcise that fact as an actual or potential interloper between my story of the one story and my readers.

It has seemed appropriate to me, in my after-consciousness of readers, in these private words, as standing perhaps in after-reading loneliness, wondering how real or unreal the spoken sense of *The Telling* might prove, kept in companionship, to provide some tokens of its authenticity as what it presents itself as being. It is as part of this provision that I testify that my story of there being essentially and ultimately but one story is my utter own. Let it not be equated with anything else! This would compromise its worth as an offering to that possibility of companionship — to the prospect of my story of the one story's retaining, in that companionship, its meaning, my meaning, of its being a story of a one story we have all to tell.

Whatever distance remains between the outreaching margins of readers' thought and mine, let it be true distance, distance between themselves, in their thought as theirs and myself in my thought as mine. This being so, nothing is lost, I think, should our approaches seem to come to nought: fate, I think, is honorable with us in the true difficulties, allowing us rebeginnings where they halt us.

September 22, 1971

Addendum

Since 'Preface for a Second Reading' was written, the subject of myth, of which I treated towards its close, has increased in popularity; the vogue of myth has acquired adherents in new fields of modernism. The spiritual effeteness of early literary modernism, which prided itself on its resort to myth, as if achieving thus primal rejuvenation, has not diminished the attraction of myth. It is not only a standard presence in the professional literary atmosphere; it has had place made for it, important place, in non-literary professional activities — such as those of art, psychology, anthropology — where need has been felt for idea-enlargements to give intellectual substance, breadth of reference, to the professional productions, beyond what has been normal within the professional limits. The quality of such addition is, unavoidably, literary.

The rôle of myth in contemporary ideology is that of a

substitute for live spiritual experience. The anthropologist Lévi-Strauss has scanned the varied record of early myth, to the most widely possible extent of data-collection, in order to resolve it into a programme of human themes to which contemporary humans might listen as to a composition presenting them to themselves with an elemental effect of plausibility: they are supposed to derive some sort of sense of reality from *this* experience. Scepticism, disbelief, cynicism, have, indeed, scared away faith in the spiritual integrity of existence. But what is myth? Myth is a tale once believed as truth; believed, it is not myth, but religion. A tale once religiously believed that has come to be called a myth is something of religion corrupted with disbelief. What are beliefs for some societies but myths for others cannot fill spiritual vacancies in the life of those others. Antique literature held myths in a state of suspension of belief, and drew some potency of spiritual excitation from their not altogether extinct or not altogether forgotten reverenced religious status. But this rummaging in the storehouse of religious or literary history for myth-matter for ideational uses is of the nature of spiritual vulgarity.

There was spiritually vulgar resort to myth in nineteen-century modernism: myth was put to work to give elegance of form to the ebulliencies of the new modern emotionalisms (as, the Wagnerian). Twentieth-century resort to myth differs from such romantic exploitation of it. It is under academic administration; it has been provided with respectabilities of special terminology. Modern myth-vision is not, however, a new educatedness in the processes of spiritual understanding; it is an educatedness in accommodation to confusions arresting the processes.

The potentialities of unwholesomeness in contemporary myth-interest are clearly perceptible when it is pursued in categorically religious domains of interest. The contemporary appetite for religion without religion becomes voracious in these domains as speculative liberalism invades them and an effort is made to maintain a compatibility between it and the formal identity 'religion'. The contemporary theological form of myth-cultivation can be seen exemplified with un-flinching pragmatism in the ideas of the academic theologian Mircea Eliade, who is also a literary fabulist dealing in mysti-fication in which the lines dividing the real from the illusory disappear. In his religious arguing of the psychological use-fulness of the world-inheritance of myth as a source of symbols to live by spiritually, the lines dividing good and evil, true and make-believe, the known and the invented, are denied actuality, in the first place. So is the modern world made possible for religion — for an art of religion. Beyond a present practice of putting myth to psycho-religious uses, this theology makes future religious success depend on new symbols of things sacred. The future hope is reduced to a profane postu-late. The principle is a sympathetic version of that which prescribes the saving of 'art' for the modern world by myth: to see the religious light is to imagine it in the dark; to make light literarily is to pretend that dark can be made into light.

Myth-vision in the T. S. Eliot sense of moribund poetic vision myth-enlivened is an optics of metaphor without relation to the faculties and functions involved in spiritual perception, the vision of spiritual meanings. It is as such an optics — an imi-tation of poetic vision — that the terms of myth have been applied outside the native ground of poetic sensitivity. By the addition of such an optics to scientific analytical perspicuity, refinements of 'poetic' analysis have been introduced where they cannot be verily domesticated — they are a written-in, a literary, supplement.

But is there a real 'poetic vision'? I have spoken of poetry as incapable of answering fully to our needs and our powers of knowing and telling the human experience to the full. But I think that there has been a reality of special vision in some poets. There are some whose minds are instinct with an assurance of there being a knowable and tellable all, even while they obey the poetic compulsion — the ordinance of poetry itself — to abbreviate truth for beauty's sake, to present visible parts of an invisible whole as if they were presenting the whole. Spiritual perception in such can overleap the 'artistic' limitations of poetry in an awareness of more to know and tell than can be poetically conceived and articulated. I view this awareness as not common among poets, as an occasional manifestation in the past, and, now, not confidently presumable anywhere.

'Real' poetic vision may be described as vision of spiritual meanings, in poets, operating outside poems, having only scanty representation in them. Explicit representation of it is more likely to be found outside poems, in the utterances of poets — and where found will be more substantial than what their poems yield of it. When it is found, in the non-poetic writing of a poet, the difficulty of giving the expression a supporting context, a form in which it will have an authority of seriousness beyond that of marginal, experimental reflection, is conspicuous. Keats and Coleridge, who must be credited with phenomenal sincerity in dedication to spiritual vision, provide illustration of this predicament. With Keats, the extra-poetic expression excited by his vehemently strong emotional persuasion of there being a more to see and say than the poetically possible came only as by flashes occurring in a state of partial blindness.

Thus wrote Keats, in statement off the poetic record, so to speak. "The World is the Vale of Soul-Making." (Soul is to be distinguished from Intelligence.) "There may be intelligences, sparks of divinity, in millions, but they are not Souls till they acquire identities, till each one is personally itself." How is this to be? "How but by the medium of a world like this?" The system is one of 'Spirit-creation'. Three 'grand materials' act upon one another: intelligence, the human heart and the World or elemental space "united in the proper action of Mind and Heart (as distinguished from intelligence or mind) on each other for the purpose of forming *the Soul or Intelli-*

gence destined to possess the sense of identity". For all the distracted quality of the expression, it reveals a genuine spiritual vision endeavoring to escape from the imprisonment in which poetic vision and poetic expression reciprocally bind each other; it attests to the realness of poetic vision where it is, as it here reveals itself to be, a straining for the vision of spiritual meanings that will not altogether compose itself to poetry's offering of a picture-making magic of words where eyes may fail. Different is the case — for instance — with Blake. He locked up his poetic vision within a siege-enclosure to keep it from the temptations of spiritual curiosity: it was tamed to know nothing beyond the myth-structure, the private cosmogony, he created for its occupancy. Keen was his poetic sight for all within this narrowly personal spirituality. Poetic vision was here held in duress to serve as a private religious vision inaccessible to outer questioning, influence, assault.

In Coleridge there was, because of the very strong element of intellectual self-consciousness in the sincerity with which he pursued the potentialities of poetic vision, a remarkable arrestment of the vision just where it fell short as practical perception of the spiritual ultimates and left the poetic tongue without powers of distinct spiritual articulation. At this point Coleridge placed his poet-powers in the care of two alternating moods, absorption in the sheer expression of physical emotions, on the one hand, and, on the other, in the exploration of the moral emotions. Restive in this, he divided himself into poet and philosopher, trying to discover a philosophic vision that could serve as an intellectually honorable spiritual extender of poetic vision. (How Wordsworth fits into this conception of Coleridge's plight is in the field of literary rather than spiritual criticism!) But Coleridge found no peace in this: there came to be for him an absolute necessity of purely religious faith in the 'perfection of human intelligence'. (This last, a word of Keat's, also.)

In Coleridge's speaking outside the borders of poetry, words reach into the heart of the problem of spiritual vision, not words in their categorically poetic aspects, but 'words select and determinate . . . that is, living words' — words in which is 'the Spirit of the living creatures'. And Reason must be known in its superiority to 'Sensibility' — 'for the greater part a quality of the nerves, and a result of individual bodily temperament'. "Alas, how many are there in this over-stimulated age, — in which the occurrence of excessive and un-healthy sensitiveness is so frequent, as even to have reversed the current meaning of the word 'nervous'." — Here Coleridge, the improver, by philosophic, then religious, stages, on poetic vision, cannot but be thinking of — among others — Coleridge the poet. As compared with Keats, Coleridge indeed labored more with intellect than 'sensibility' in the proposing of the crucial terms of the finalities of visionary experience. For Coleridge, Reason is the leading member of the spiritual college. He scolds those who talk big of the Spirit and inveigh against reason: "it is enduring and penetrating steel, even the Sword of the Spirit." "Our great Hooker says", he ad-vances, that Reason "is a direct aspect of Truth, an inward beholding" — the very process of final vision.

Keats, in his rather pagan overreaching of the limits of poetic vision, looks askance at the Christian view of the human spiritual condition. Coleridge, in his effort to construe a religious view of things spiritual, is not content with thrusts of the imagination into the region outlying the scene of poetic thought. He must have a definable, accessible practicality of spiritual principle, a law of spiritual vision by which to know where to find the spiritual meanings for the language of truth. He, wearing the philosopher identity only incidentally, chose for his destination a Christianity so purified as to be the unrejectable religious ultimate. One may think of Coleridge as a poet adopting the austere extreme of vision of a cleric with a guilty personal sense of the lenient limitations of poetic vision. Speaking of all the misconceptions of 'the eternity of the Supreme Being' from the point of view of his rationally pure Christianity, those of Aristotle and Plotinus included, he dismisses them all as necessarily false. "For if they were true, the idea must lose the sole ground of its reality" — being not "the premiss with which alone religion is concerned. The very subject would be changed. It would no longer be the God in whom be believed, but a stoical Fate, or the supernal one of Plotinus, to whom neither intelligence nor self-consciousness, nor life, nor even being can be attributed; or lastly the World itself, the indivisible and only substance (*substantia una et unica*) of Spinoza . . .'

Yet besides straining for theological purity of conception of essentialities and ultimates, to polemical ferocity, nearly, Coleridge kept in the midst of this a personal spirituality of vision itself very pure, of a free force, exceeding in intensity in him all that was of categorical identity — a force that led the way in much of his thinking. It is ever evident in his expressed perceptions of the nature of the linguistic proprieties, as in the quoted comment on 'nervous', and in how he takes up words for use and lays them into his sentences. He does not go far in any kind or form of expression without using some word in a way that presents it newly energetic with distinction. (Few of the English literary line have known words with an acuity of consciousness of their potentialities of use such as his.)

As to that free force of vision of which I have spoken, I shall quote two sayings of his in which he seems to me to act in freedom from sponsorship of poetic and philosophic and theological forms of vision-experience (in which forms of expression condition the vision!) — to express vision-experience with accents of direct personal presence and total personal assumption of linguistic responsibleness. These have impressed me more than what I have already quoted here of his saying, as manifesting this quality, in that they have each a point of close meeting with two sayings of mine, one in that part of the Preface in which I give the personal history of *The Telling*,

and the other in *The Telling* proper itself. I can seem to be
making my mode of saying a canon! But I mean only that I
know that such coincidence as there is assures the non-
categorical, the personal, sponsorship of the sayings of each.

What I shall first quote has correspondence with words of
mine as to the personal origins of *The Telling*. The theme of
what I say is expressed in "I have made visits to the human
actualness of my being." Coleridge has written:

. . . the greater part of mankind cannot be prevailed upon to visit
themselves sometimes; but according to the saying of Solomon,
The eyes of the fool are on the ends of the earth.

Next: to quote a phrase of mine formed in the privacy of
intellectual care to describe a certain vision-experience of mine
to my personal truest. It comes in passage *22* of *The Telling*.
I speak of "a common potentiality of imagining back to the
all-antecedent reality". In passage *24* there is another reference
to this reality: "We see, or we shall see, an all-familiar One-
image — our Before!" Coleridge speaks of 'an antecedent
unity'. This phrase is patently all his own, animated by his
intellectual concentration and spiritual vigor, not responsive to
accepted special conditions of utterance. Having named an
all-encompassing presiding reality, according to thought on its
nature in the midst of a vision of it, he unfolds in further
words what he sees implicit in its nature. He names and describes three potencies of the unity, three key distinctions,
different integral constants of it. These are: THE LAW, as
empowering, THE WORD, as informing, THE SPIRIT, as
actuating. There is a suggestion of theological environment,
and Formal Religion is a friend (all that I have quoted here,
of Coleridge's, is from *Aids to Reflection*). But one feels an
immediate personal authenticity of experience, thought, word.
The words match his prescription — "words select and determinate . . . living words".

I have not dwelt on Coleridge as a model. Such speaking

as I have quoted, of his, with other that might be quoted for its success as free expression of free recognitions, has no center, does not gather into a self-consistent, self-confirming whole of sense; he has not achieved a general position, identified the common ground of truth. But he exemplifies flight from the special ground — in his case, the special ground of literature. What I have added by way of epilogue may help to clarify the relation between the general human problems that my book brings forward and the problems of the special worlds wherein these problems are subjected to special treatment. The world of literature, which tends to blend itself with other special worlds, and which other special worlds tend to blend into themselves, equates itself with the general world and regards itself, and is regarded traditionally, as very deeply occupied with general human problems, and as especially wise in them. But the problems of this world are literary problems — and those of other special worlds are likewise reductions of the general problems to the interest-norms of each. In the literary area of occupation with problems, the poetic preoccupations seem to transcend *in themselves* the special-interest character of the world of which they are part. Coleridge's efforts of escape from the stricture of literary spirituality make the differences between commitment to a special orientation and struggle for a general reality of reference in what one is doing, and of meaning in what one is saying, dramatically plain. His transcendencies are real, though fragmentary. He shows that it is possible to keep touching the real upper level, or outer bounds — and keep oneself from falling back, or springing back, onto the peculiar ground of special vision, special understanding, special speaking, with norms of un-conventionality the only escape from indurated and indurating norms, and, from 'truth' (truth modified into untrue existence in the special world), 'myth' the only one (myth modified into improbable existence there, also).

February 29, 1972